Welcome to Issue 10 of Martial Arts Magazine Australia.

As we approach 2026, we stand on the threshold of something extraordinary—the Year of the Fire Horse. This convergence of elemental power occurs only once every sixty years in the Chinese zodiac, bringing with it the spirit of unbridled passion, courage, and determination. It seems fitting, then, that our tenth issue opens with the legend of Red Hare, the magnificent crimson stallion who carried China's greatest warriors across ancient battlefields.

The story of Red Hare and the warriors Lü Bu and Guan Yu offers us more than historical fascination. It presents a timeless question for every martial artist: What defines true excellence? Is it raw power and technical mastery, or is it the integration of skill with character, loyalty, and honour? Through these ancient tales, we're reminded that the martial arts journey is as much about cultivating virtue as it is about perfecting technique.

This issue showcases the remarkable diversity of our martial arts community. From Wing Chun's internal power development to the championship spirit forged at Shaolin Kempo, from women breaking barriers in martial arts workshops to senior practitioners honouring decades of experience—each article reflects a different facet of what it means to walk the martial path.

You'll find deeply personal reflections alongside practical guidance, philosophical insights paired with hands-on instruction. Our contributors—from established masters to dedicated students—share their unique perspectives on courage, teaching, mentorship, and the enduring question of identity: "I am a martial artist." What does that truly mean?

We're particularly proud to feature articles that highlight the foundations of our practice—literally, in "From the Ground Up," and philosophically, in explorations of karatedo and traditional values. These pieces remind us that beneath the surface diversity of styles and systems lies a shared commitment to growth, discipline, and the pursuit of excellence.

As always, Martial Arts Magazine Australia remains proudly ad-free, allowing us to focus entirely on content that serves the martial arts community. We're not here to sell you anything except ideas, inspiration, and the collective wisdom of practitioners who've dedicated their lives to these arts.

The Year of the Fire Horse invites us to embody passion and determination in our training. May this issue kindle that fire within you, remind you why you began this journey, and inspire you to continue with renewed purpose and commitment.

Thank you for being part of our community. Your support makes this magazine possible, and your dedication to the martial arts makes it meaningful.

Train well,
Vanessa McKay
Editor-in-Chief
Martial Arts Magazine Australia

All content published in MAMA (Marital Arts Magazine Australia), including articles, images, and other media, is the property of the magazine and is protected by copyright law. The author retains the copyright to their individual work, but by submitting their work to MAMA, they grant the magazine an exclusive, perpetual, and irrevocable license to publish and distribute their work in all formats, including print, digital, and online media. No part of MAMA may be reproduced, distributed, or transmitted in any form or by any means, including photocopying, recording, or other electronic or mechanical methods, without the prior written permission of the magazine.

MAMA respects the intellectual property rights of others and expects its contributors and readers to do the same. If you believe that your copyrighted work has been used in a way that constitutes copyright infringement, please contact MAMA immediately. Additionally, any use of MAMA trademarks, including the magazine's name and logo, without prior written authorization from the magazine, is prohibited.

MAMA strives to showcase original and unique content, and as such, does not accept any submissions that have been previously published or that are under consideration by other publications. By submitting their work to MAWA Magazine, the author confirms that their work is original and has not been published or submitted elsewhere.

In addition, MAMA reserves the right to edit all submissions for grammar, style, and clarity, and to reject any submission that does not adhere to the magazine's standards or guidelines. The magazine also reserves the right to remove or modify any content that is deemed inappropriate or offensive, at its sole discretion.
MAMA acknowledges and respects the rights of all individuals and groups and will not publish any content that promotes hate speech, discrimination, or any form of violence. The magazine also respects the privacy of its contributors and readers and will not share or sell any personal information to third parties without prior written consent. By submitting their work to MAMA, the author agrees to abide by these copyright specifics and to grant the magazine the rights outlined in this statement. The author also certifies that their work is original and does not infringe on the rights of any third party. MAMA reserves the right to modify these copyright specifics at any time without prior notice.

If you have any questions or concerns regarding these copyright specifics, please contact MAMA at info@martialartsmagazineaustralia.com

CONTENTS

The Fire Horse Legend	5
Wing Chun Ling Tung Gong	19
Building Courage	24
From the Ground Up	32
Women in Martial Arts Workshop	41
Beyond the Bruise	45
Champions Made at Shaolin Kempo	50
Honouring Experience	53
I am a Martial Artisit	61
My Outlook on Karatedo	64
A Martial Artists Essential Guide	67
He Toa Takitini	73
Teaching with Understanding	79
My Martial Arts Mentor	89
The Sham-an	94

The Fire Horse Legend
Red Hare and China's Greatest Warriors

As 2026 approaches, we stand at the threshold of the Year of the Fire Horse, a convergence of elemental power that occurs only once every sixty years in the Chinese zodiac. The Fire Horse (火馬, huǒ mǎ) represents the fusion of unbridled freedom with passionate intensity, the marriage of speed with determination, and the embodiment of a spirit that refuses to be contained or controlled.

In the rich tapestry of Chinese martial history, no legend captures this Fire Horse essence more perfectly than the tale of Red Hare (赤兔馬, Chìtù mǎ). The magnificent crimson steed whose hooves thundered across ancient battlefields, carrying the greatest warriors China has ever known. This is not merely a story about a horse and its riders. It is a testament to the values that define martial arts excellence: loyalty that endures beyond death, courage that faces impossible odds, honour that cannot be compromised, and the relentless spirit to Ascend, Persevere, and Triumph.

The story of Red Hare emerges from the twilight years of the Eastern Han Dynasty, during the tumultuous period known as the Three Kingdoms era (169-280 CE). China, once united under a single imperial banner, had fractured into warring states, and it was in this crucible of conflict that legends were forged.

Red Hare's name comes from the literal Chinese—chì meaning 'red' or 'crimson,' and tù meaning 'hare' or 'rabbit.' This magnificent stallion earned its name from a coat described in the classical text Romance of the Three Kingdoms as "of uniform colour like glowing-sun red, not a hair of another colour." The horse embodied fire itself, a living flame that moved with the legendary speed of the hare.

Historical records, specifically the Records of the Three Kingdoms (Sanguozhi) compiled by the historian Chen Shou in the third century, confirm that such a horse existed. The annotation to this historical text preserves a saying that echoed through the ages: "Among men, Lü Bu; Among steeds, Red Hare" (人中有呂布，馬中有赤兔). This single line elevates both warrior and horse to the pinnacle of their respective realms. The ultimate fighter riding the ultimate mount.

The horse was said to possess supernatural abilities. Romance of the Three Kingdoms describes Red Hare as capable of "running one thousand li in a single day" (approximately 500 kilometres), an impossible feat that speaks to the legend's symbolic power rather than literal truth. The horse could "gallop across cities and leap over moats," making cavalry charges that seemed to defy the laws of physics. In the hands of a master warrior, Red Hare became more than transportation; it became an extension of the fighter's will, a living weapon that amplified human potential to mythic proportions.

Lü Bu (呂布, died 199 CE) stands as one of the most formidable warriors in Chinese history. Nicknamed "Flying General" (飛將軍, Fēi Jiāngjūn) for his unmatched martial prowess, Lü Bu specialised in archery and horse-riding, possessed extraordinary physical strength, and commanded respect and fear in equal measure across the fractured kingdoms.

In Romance of the Three Kingdoms, the bond between Lü Bu and Red Hare begins with a gift from the tyrannical warlord Dong Zhuo. The horse becomes the physical manifestation of Lü Bu's power—a creature as untameable and dangerous as the warrior himself. Together, they became legendary.

The Battle of Hulao Gate: An Excerpt
One of the most famous passages from Romance of the Three Kingdoms describes Lü Bu's entrance at the Battle of Hulao Gate, where a coalition of warlords had gathered to challenge Dong Zhuo's tyranny:

"From the Sishui Gate came forth a general, riding a magnificent steed. He wore a three-pronged purple-gold crown, and a hundred-flowered robe. Upon his body was the armour of a Tang warrior, and at his waist a jewelled belt. His mount was the Red Hare horse. In his hand, he wielded a mighty halberd.

"Who dares challenge me?" cried Lü Bu, his voice like thunder rolling across the plain. His Red Hare pawed the earth, sending up clouds of dust that seemed to burn like crimson smoke in the morning sun. The assembled warriors, men of courage who had never known fear, felt their hearts quail. For here was the Flying General, and beneath him, the Fire Horse that had never known defeat."

In this battle, Lü Bu faced three of the coalition's greatest heroes simultaneously— the oath brothers Liu Bei, Guan Yu, and Zhang Fei. Though three against one, Lü Bu on Red Hare fought them to a standstill, demonstrating such overwhelming skill that even combined, these legendary warriors could barely hold their ground.

Yet Lü Bu's story serves as a cautionary tale for martial artists. Despite his unmatched physical prowess and his legendary mount, Lü Bu's character flaws ultimately led to his downfall. He was notorious for his instability, switching allegiances erratically and betraying those who trusted him. He assassinated his adoptive father Ding Yuan, then later turned on his new master Dong Zhuo. His pattern of betrayal earned him the distrust of all, even as they feared his martial skills.

The Records of the Three Kingdoms notes: "Although Lü Bu is described in historical and fictional sources as an exceptionally mighty warrior, he was also notorious for his unstable behaviour. He switched allegiances erratically and freely betrayed his allies. He was always suspicious of others and could not control his subordinates. All these factors ultimately led to his downfall."

In 199 CE, Lü Bu was captured at the Battle of Xiapi by the warlord Cao Cao. Despite his legendary status, Lü Bu was executed, his inability to inspire loyalty proving more fatal than any warrior's blade. Even Red Hare could not save a man who had betrayed honour itself.

The lesson for martial artists is clear: physical prowess alone does not define a true warrior. Without honour, without loyalty, without the wisdom to lead and inspire others, even the mightiest fighter is ultimately hollow. Lü Bu could defeat any opponent in single combat, but he could not conquer his own character flaws. He had mastered the external arts of war but neglected the internal cultivation of virtue.

After Lü Bu's death, Red Hare passed into the hands of Cao Cao, the brilliant and ruthless warlord who controlled much of northern China. Cao Cao had also captured one of Lü Bu's greatest enemies: Guan Yu (關羽, died 220 CE), the sworn brother of Liu Bei and one of the Three Heroes who had fought Lü Bu at Hulao Gate.

Where Lü Bu embodied raw martial power, Guan Yu represented the complete warrior—a man of both incredible fighting skill and unshakeable moral character. Known for his loyalty to his oath brothers, his sense of righteousness, and his personal honour, Guan Yu would eventually be deified as the God of War (關帝, Guān Dì), becoming one of the most widely worshipped figures in Chinese culture.

Guan Yu was instantly recognisable on any battlefield. He had a distinctive red face (said to show his fierce loyalty and righteous anger), a magnificent long beard that earned him the nickname "Lord of the Beautiful Beard" (美髯公, Měi Rán Gōng), and he wielded the legendary Green Dragon Crescent Blade (青龍偃月刀, Qīnglóng Yǎnyuè Dāo)—a massive halberd said to weigh 82 Chinese pounds, which he could swing with devastating effect.

The Gift of Red Hare: An Excerpt

In Romance of the Three Kingdoms (Chapters 25-26), Cao Cao attempts to win Guan Yu's loyalty by showering him with gifts and honours. But Guan Yu remains steadfastly loyal to his sworn brother Liu Bei, from whom he has been separated by the chaos of war. The pivotal moment comes when Cao Cao presents him with Red Hare:

"Cao Cao summoned Guan Yu to his hall and said, 'General, I have obtained a magnificent treasure—the Red Hare horse that once belonged to Lü Bu. Among all the steeds in the realm, none can match its speed and spirit. I present it to you as a token of my esteem.'

"Guan Yu bowed low in gratitude and said, 'My lord's generosity overwhelms me. This noble beast will allow me to serve you with greater efficiency. Should I learn of my brother Liu Bei's whereabouts, I will be able to reach him more swiftly.'

"Cao Cao's face darkened at these words, but he dared not rebuke Guan Yu. For even as the general accepted the gift, he made clear where his true loyalty lay."

Guan Yu was instantly recognisable on any This moment crystallises Guan Yu's character. Even while separated from his sworn brother and offered every inducement to change allegiance, Guan Yu's honour remained uncompromised. He accepts the horse not out of greed or temptation, but because it will help him fulfill his duty—to return to Liu Bei.

The Gift of Red Hare: An Excerpt

In Romance of the Three Kingdoms (Chapters 25-26), Cao Cao attempts to win Guan Yu's loyalty by showering him with gifts and honours. But Guan Yu remains steadfastly loyal to his sworn brother Liu Bei, from whom he has been separated by the chaos of war. The pivotal moment comes when Cao Cao presents him with Red Hare:

"Cao Cao summoned Guan Yu to his hall and said, 'General, I have obtained a magnificent treasure—the Red Hare horse that once belonged to Lü Bu. Among all the steeds in the realm, none can match its speed and spirit. I present it to you as a token of my esteem.'

"Guan Yu bowed low in gratitude and said, 'My lord's generosity overwhelms me. This noble beast will allow me to serve you with greater efficiency. Should I learn of my brother Liu Bei's whereabouts, I will be able to reach him more swiftly.'

"Cao Cao's face darkened at these words, but he dared not rebuke Guan Yu. For even as the general accepted the gift, he made clear where his true loyalty lay."

This moment crystallises Guan Yu's character. Even while separated from his sworn brother and offered every inducement to change allegiance, Guan Yu's honour remained uncompromised. He accepts the horse not out of greed or temptation, but because it will help him fulfill his duty—to return to Liu Bei.

Shortly after receiving Red Hare, Guan Yu learned of Liu Bei's location. True to his word, he departed from Cao Cao's service, embarking on the legendary "Journey of a Thousand Li" (千里走單騎, Qiānlǐ Zǒu Dān Qí). On this journey, he faced five mountain passes, each guarded by Cao Cao's officers who tried to prevent his passage. At each pass, Guan Yu defeated the guards, killing six generals and clearing five passes, all while protecting Liu Bei's family members who travelled with him.

The Journey of a Thousand Li: An Excerpt

The Romance describes one of these encounters:
"At the first pass, Kong Xiu stepped forward, barring the way with his spear. 'General Guan, you cannot leave without Lord Cao's written permission,' he declared.

"Guan Yu's eyes blazed like molten iron. 'I have served Lord Cao well, and I leave with honour. Stand aside or face the consequences of your obstinacy.'

"Kong Xiu raised his weapon. 'Then you force my hand!'

"Red Hare surged forward like a crimson thunderbolt. Guan Yu's Green Dragon Blade rose and fell in a single, perfect arc. Kong Xiu's head flew from his shoulders before he could strike a single blow. The Red Hare did not even break stride as it carried Guan Yu through the pass, the guards scattering like leaves before a storm."

This legendary journey established Guan Yu's reputation not just as a warrior, but as the embodiment of righteousness (義, yì) the Confucian virtue that encompasses loyalty, honour, justice, and moral courage. With Red Hare beneath him, Guan Yu became unstoppable, but his true strength came from his unwavering principles.

The Death of Loyalty
In 220 CE, Guan Yu met his end. Captured by the forces of the warlord Sun Quan during a military campaign, Guan Yu refused all offers to change his allegiance and was executed. According to Romance of the Three Kingdoms, when Red Hare was presented to Sun Quan, the horse refused to eat. The Fire Horse, it was said, died of grief for its master. Choosing death over serving another.

This poignant ending transforms Red Hare from merely a powerful war horse into a symbol of loyalty itself. The Fire Horse, which had carried both the mighty Lü Bu and the righteous Guan Yu, made its final choice, demonstrating that true loyalty transcends death, and that honour matters more than survival.

Loyalty(忠 , Zhōng): The Foundation of Character
Guan Yu's unwavering loyalty to Liu Bei, even in the face of death, represents the highest ideal of martial character. In our modern practice, loyalty manifests as:
•Commitment to our teachers and training lineage: Respecting those who have passed down knowledge to us.
•Dedication to our training partners: supporting each other's growth rather than competing destructively.
• Fidelity to our own principles: maintaining our values even when it would be easier to compromise.
•Honour towards our opponents: treating every encounter with respect, whether in the dojo or in life.

Lü Bu's betrayals serve as the negative example, raw power without loyalty ultimately leads to isolation and defeat. A martial artist without loyalty is merely a fighter; with loyalty, they become a warrior.

Righteousness (義, Yì): The Compass of Action
Guan Yu's righteousness went beyond simple rule-following. It was an internalised moral compass that guided all his actions. For martial artists, righteousness means:
•Standing up for what is right, even when it costs us personally.
•Using our skills responsibly: understanding that martial arts training comes with ethical obligations.
• Protecting the vulnerable: using our strength to defend those who cannot defend themselves.
•Maintaining integrity: ensuring our actions align with our professed values.

Courage (勇, Yǒng): The Fire Within
Both warriors showed extraordinary physical courage, but the legend teaches us that true courage encompasses more than fearlessness in combat.
•The courage to face our weaknesses in training, acknowledging where we need to improve.
• The courage to be vulnerable with our teachers and training partners.
 The courage to stand alone when necessary, like Guan Yu at the five passes.
•The courage to show restraint: Knowing when not to fight requires as much courage as engaging in combat.

Perseverance (恆, Héng): The Long Road
Guan Yu's thousand-li journey—fighting through five passes, protecting innocents, never wavering from his goal—exemplifies perseverance. The Fire Horse's ability to run vast distances symbolises the endurance required in martial arts:
•Daily practice, even when progress seems invisible.
• Training through injury and setback, adapting but never quitting.

- Lifetime commitment to continuous improvement.
- Patience with the process; understanding that mastery is measured in decades, not weeks.

Excellence (精, Jīng): The Pursuit of Perfection
Both warriors were renowned not just for being good, but for being exceptional. The saying "Among men, Lü Bu; Among steeds, Red Hare" captures this pursuit of excellence:
- Attention to detail in every technique, every form, every movement.
- Never settling for "good enough" when better is possible.
- Refining the basics until they become extraordinary.
- Understanding that excellence is a journey, not a destination.

From Warrior to Deity
After his death, Guan Yu's legend only grew. During the Sui Dynasty (581-618 CE), he was first honored as a martial saint. By the Ming Dynasty (1368-1644), emperors had elevated him to the status of deity, and he was officially recognized as Guandi (關帝), the God of War.

This deification was unprecedented for a historical figure. Guan Yu became one of the most widely worshipped deities in Chinese culture, venerated not only as a god of war but also as:
- God of Righteousness: Representing moral courage and integrity.
- God of Loyalty: Embodying unwavering dedication.
- God of Wealth: Believed to bring prosperity to honest merchants.
- Protector deity: Guarding against evil spirits and negative influences.

Thousands of temples dedicated to Guan Yu exist across China, Taiwan, Hong Kong, Macau, Vietnam, South Korea, and Japan. Wherever Chinese communities established themselves, Guan Yu temples followed. Today, he remains one of the most popular deities in Chinese folk religion.

Guan Yu in the Martial Arts World
For martial artists, Guan Yu holds special significance. Walk into virtually any traditional Chinese martial arts school, whether practicing kung fu, tai chi, or other disciplines, and you will probably find a shrine or statue of Guan Yu. His presence serves multiple purposes:

Spiritual Protection

Martial arts schools maintain Guan Yu shrines to invoke his protective presence. Practitioners believe he guards the school from negative energy, prevents injuries during training, and watches over students during competitions. Before important training sessions or demonstrations, students may bow to Guan Yu's image, asking for his blessing and protection.

Moral Exemplar
More importantly, Guan Yu serves as a constant reminder of the values martial artists should embody. His image is typically showing his red face, long beard, and the Green Dragon Crescent Blade reminds students that:
- Technical skill must be paired with moral character.
- Loyalty to teachers and training brothers is paramount.
- Righteousness should guide all actions.
- Martial power carries ethical responsibility.

Many traditional schools perform ceremonies before Guan Yu's shrine during significant events:

- Student initiation: New students may bow before Guan Yu when formally entering the school, symbolising their commitment to the martial path.
- Belt promotions: Advanced ranks may be conferred before his image, emphasizing that rank comes with increased moral responsibility
- New Year celebrations: offerings of fruit, incense, and tea are presented to invoke blessings for the coming year.
- Memorial ceremonies: honouring deceased masters or significant historical events.

Even for martial artists who don't practice traditional Chinese styles or maintain religious shrines, the Guan Yu ideal remains relevant. Modern martial arts culture, influenced heavily by Mixed Martial Arts and sport competition, sometimes emphasises winning above all else. Guan Yu reminds us of older, deeper values:

Victory with Honour: Guan Yu defeated his enemies, but he did so according to principles. He gave Kong Xiu a chance to stand aside. He protected innocents during his journey. Modern martial artists can ask themselves: "Am I pursuing victory at any cost, or am I winning with honour?"

Loyalty Over Advancement: Guan Yu refused Cao Cao's offers of rank and riches to stay loyal to Liu Bei. Modern practitioners face similar choices: staying with a traditional teacher versus jumping to flashier gyms, maintaining relationships with training partners versus constantly seeking "better" sparring partners. Guan Yu chose loyalty, even when it seemed to limit his opportunities.

Service Over Self: Guan Yu saw his martial skill as a tool for serving his lord and protecting others, not as a means of personal aggrandisement. This perspective transforms martial arts from ego-gratification into service—teaching younger students, helping training partners improve, using our skills to protect our communities.

Character as Foundation: perhaps most importantly, Guan Yu represents the integration of martial skill with moral character. Lü Bu was the superior fighter—he fought three heroes simultaneously at Hulao Gate. But Guan Yu became the God of War, while Lü Bu is remembered as a cautionary tale. The difference? Character.

Lessons for 2026 and Beyond
As we enter the Year of the Fire Horse in 2026, the legend of Red Hare offers martial artists a powerful framework for understanding our practice and our path.

The Fire Horse Spirit
The Fire Horse in Chinese astrology represents:
- Unbridled passion: the fire element intensifies the horse's natural enthusiasm.
- Independence: the willingness to forge one's own path.
- Dynamic energy: constant movement and action.
- Courage: facing challenges head-on.
- Speed and determination: swift action towards goals.

These qualities, when properly channelled, can elevate our martial arts practice. Red Hare demonstrates what happens when these qualities serve worthy purposes and righteous masters.

Which Warrior Will You Be?
The legend presents us with two paths, two ways of harnessing the Fire Horse spirit:
The Path of Lü Bu: raw power without wisdom, skill without character, ambition without honour. This path leads to short-term victories but ultimate defeat. Lü Bu could defeat anyone in single combat, but he died betrayed and alone.

The Path of Guan Yu: power integrated with principle, skill guided by wisdom, ambition tempered by loyalty. This path may involve temporary setbacks (Guan Yu was separated from Liu Bei, had to serve Cao Cao, faced five passes) but leads to a lasting legacy. Guan Yu became a god.

The choice is not about whether to be strong, skilled, or ambitious—the Fire Horse spirit demands all these things. The choice is about what guides that strength, how we apply that skill, and what purpose our ambition serves.

As we move through 2026, consider these questions in your martial arts practice:
Am I cultivating character alongside technique? It's easy to focus solely on physical skills—the perfect kick, the fastest punch, the most submissions. But are you also developing patience, humility, and respect? Are you becoming a better person through your training, or just a more dangerous one?
Do I demonstrate loyalty to my teachers and training partners? In the age of YouTube tutorials and gym-hopping, loyalty can seem outdated. But Guan Yu shows us that loyalty builds something deeper than technique—it builds trust, community, and lineage. How do you demonstrate loyalty in your practice?

Am I pursuing excellence or just adequacy? "Among men, Lü Bu; Among steeds, Red Hare"—are you content with being good enough, or are you striving to be exceptional? This doesn't mean comparing yourself to others, but rather asking if you're giving your full effort to become the best version of yourself.

Do my actions align with my principles? Guan Yu's righteousness wasn't theoretical—it guided every action. When you face challenges in training or life, do your choices reflect your stated values? Or do you compromise when it's convenient? Am I willing to persevere through obstacles? Guan Yu's thousand-li journey wasn't a straight line—it involved five passes, six generals, constant obstacles. Your martial arts journey will have similar challenges. Are you committed for the long haul?

Do I use my skills responsibly? Both warriors were capable of tremendous violence, but Guan Yu used his power judiciously, while Lü Bu used his recklessly. How do you exercise restraint? How do you ensure your skills serve positive purposes?

The Year of the Fire Horse comes once every sixty years. Most of us will experience it only once or twice in our lifetime. This makes 2026 a unique opportunity, a cosmic prompt to examine our martial arts practice with fresh eyes.
Use this year as a catalyst for transformation:
•Recommit to your training with Fire Horse intensity
•Examine and refine your character with honest self-reflection
•Deepen your loyalty to your teachers and training community
•Pursue excellence with renewed dedication
•Recommit to righteousness in all your actions

The legend of Red Hare and its warriors has endured for over eighteen centuries because it speaks to something fundamental about the martial spirit. It tells us that physical prowess alone is never enough. That technique without character is empty. That power without principle is ultimately self-destructive.

Red Hare, the Fire Horse, represents pure potential—tremendous speed, power, and spirit. But the story shows us that this potential can take two paths. Under Lü Bu, the Fire Horse became an instrument of betrayal and instability. Under Guan Yu, it became a vehicle for righteousness and loyalty.

Each of us has our own Fire Horse. Our potential, our energy, our martial spirit. The question is not whether we have this power (we all do), but rather who is riding. Are we guided by the Lü Bu within us—seeking glory, switching loyalties when convenient, prioritizing personal advancement above all? Or are we guided by the Guan Yu within us—committed to principles, loyal to those we've sworn to support, using our power for righteous purposes?

As martial artists in the twenty-first century, we stand at an interesting crossroads. Modern training methods have never been better—we understand biomechanics, sports science, nutrition, and psychology in ways previous generations could only dream of. We can watch and learn from fighters across the globe, study techniques from every tradition, cross-train in multiple disciplines.

Yet in this abundance of physical knowledge, we risk losing something the ancients understood: that the martial arts are fundamentally about character development, not just combat efficiency. The legends endure not because Lü Bu and Guan Yu were the most skilled fighters of their time (though they were), but because their stories teach us about the kind of people we should strive to become.

Guan Yu was deified not for his combat record but for his character. His unwavering loyalty, his uncompromising righteousness, his courage in the face of death, his commitment to his principles—these are the qualities that transformed a warrior into a god. These are the qualities that thousands of martial arts schools across the world honour when they maintain his shrine.

The Fire Horse year reminds us to harness our passion, to channel our intensity, to ride our potential with both courage and wisdom. It calls us to Ascend—constantly climbing toward greater skill and deeper understanding. It demands that we Persevere—maintaining our commitment through obstacles and setbacks. And it promises that if we do these things with honour and integrity, we will Triumph—not just over opponents, but over our own limitations.

So as 2026 approaches, as the Fire Horse year gallops toward us with all its passionate intensity, ask yourself: What kind of rider will you be? Will you harness this energy with wisdom and righteousness, or will you let it carry you toward betrayal and defeat?

The choice, like the legendary Red Hare itself, is powerful, is free, and is ultimately yours.

May you ride with honour. May you journey with loyalty. May you fight with righteousness. And may the spirit of the Fire Horse carry you swiftly on the warrior's path.

Wing Chun Ling Tung Gong
A Living Tradition of Health and Martial Power
by Sifu David Richardson

In the rich history of Wing Chun, most people know the name of Grandmaster Ip Man. Fewer are aware of the lesser-known but profoundly important internal training method he preserved: Wing Chun Ling Tung Gong. This rare system was entrusted to his private disciple, Grandmaster Gregory Choi, who passed it on at the end of his teaching life to one final student — David Richardson of Kung Fu Southside in Brisbane, Australia.

A Chance Encounter

Sifu Richardson's journey toward Ling Tung Gong began not in a training hall, but in a Yum Cha restaurant in Brisbane in 2016. There he met Grandmaster Choi, who overheard him speaking about Wing Chun. At the time, Richardson was a student of Grandmaster William Cheung. The two struck up a conversation that grew into a friendship, and over many meals together, Grandmaster Choi shared stories of his time with Ip Man in early 1950s Hong Kong.

Although Grandmaster often said he no longer taught, he eventually told Sifu Dave that if he got GM Cheung's blessing, he would accept him as his closed-door disciple (關門弟子) — the last student he would ever teach. After deep reflection, Richardson made the difficult decision, and in January 2019, he formally began training under Grandmaster Choi.

What is Ling Tung Gong?

Wing Chun Ling Tung Gong is a method of Qigong within the Wing Chun system. Its purpose is to harmonise Qi, nourish the organs, and strengthen the body from within. It balances 36 Gong forms — some slow and restorative, others explosive and dynamic — creating a complete system that supports both health and martial effectiveness.

Unlike ordinary exercise, Ling Tung Gong works at the energetic level, addressing stress, fatigue, poor posture, and lifestyle-related illness by restoring balance to the whole person. It strengthens immunity, calms the mind, and promotes longevity, while also developing the relaxed, spring-like power that makes Wing Chun unique.

The name carries rich meaning. 靈 (Ling) suggests spirit, alertness, and effectiveness, while 通 (Tung) means to connect and to know well. Together, they describe a natural and effective path of training that leads to abundant health, martial skill, and a deeper harmony with life.

Health and Longevity

Where modern fitness often works only on the surface — muscles and endurance — Ling Tung Gong works at the root. The Yin practices calm the nervous system, support digestion, and nourish the organs, while the Yang practices build strength, align the body, and train

Sifu David Richardson

explosive release of energy. This balance not only prevents illness but also reverses the effects of stress, overwork, and sedentary living.

Sifu Richardson has seen students and patients benefit with reduced pain, improved posture, greater energy, and a calmer mind. "Perhaps most importantly," he says, "people begin to see themselves differently. They realise that their body, breath, and mind are connected, and that balance in one area brings balance in all."

Sifu Richardson has seen students and patients benefit with reduced pain, improved posture, greater energy, and a calmer mind. "Perhaps most importantly," he says, "people begin to see themselves differently. They realise that their body, breath, and mind are connected, and that balance in one area brings balance in all."

Healing and Prevention

In Chinese tradition, martial arts and healing go hand in hand. Ling Tung Gong embodies this balance. Prevention is placed above cure: training harmonises Qi and strengthens the body so that illness is less likely to arise. The system also preserves Dit Da practices (traditional trauma medicine) passed from Ip Man which ensure that recovery and protection are part of the complete art.

Transmission and Preservation

Sifu Richardson explains: "My teacher, Grandmaster Choi, entrusted me with Ling Tung Gong as his final disciple. I see my role not as ownership, but as custodianship — to preserve what has been given to me and pass it on faithfully. The practice strengthens the body, calms the mind, and cultivates balance. Its true value is not only in martial skill, but in improving health and quality of life."

Transmission and Preservation

Sifu Richardson explains: "My teacher, Grandmaster Choi, entrusted me with Ling Tung Gong as his final disciple. I see my role not as ownership, but as custodianship — to preserve what has been given to me and pass it on faithfully. The practice strengthens the body, calms the mind, and cultivates balance. Its true value is not only in martial skill, but in improving health and quality of life."
Currently, Sifu Richardson is the only person entrusted by Grandmaster Choi to teach Ling Tung Gong. He offers private tuition, seminars, and workshops, while also preparing an upcoming book to preserve the system's theory and practice.

"Face-to-face teaching will always remain the heart of transmission," he says. "Books and digital resources can provide context, but the depth of Ling Tung Gong can only be experienced directly under guidance."

For martial artists, it refines structure and power. For everyday people, it offers health, resilience, and longevity. Above all, it is a living tradition — a gift from the past, safeguarded for the future.

"I am simply a custodian. My role is to preserve what I have been given and to pass it on faithfully."

The Future of Ling Tung Gong

Sifu Richardson sees the future as a balance between preservation and sharing. Closed-door discipleship ensures the art remains intact for serious students, while workshops, seminars, and his upcoming book will allow more people to access its health and longevity benefits. Carefully curated digital content may also help raise awareness, but always with the reminder that the art is best learned in person.

Does Ling Tung Gong belong only to martial artists? Sifu Dave believes its value is wider. For martial practitioners, it refines power and structure. For the broader public, it offers relief from the stresses and imbalances of modern life.

A Final Word

"Wing Chun Ling Tung Gong is not just a martial art or a health exercise," Sifu Dave says. "It is a living tradition that unites both. It is a gift from the past, entrusted to us in the present, and preserved for the future.

My hope is that those who encounter it will find not only martial skill, but health, balance, and a deeper connection to life itself."

Media enquiries and seminar requests:
sifu@kungfusouthside.com.au
www.kungfusouthside.com.au

" A Man should always think of the source of the water as he drinks it."

Grandmaster Ip Man

Image by Sophie Walster

Building Courage, Teaching Respect
How Martial Arts Addresses Bullying

by Don McKay

As a karate instructor who has taught children for over twenty years, I've witnessed countless transformations. Shy children discovering their voice. Anxious children finding confidence. Aggressive children learning self-control. But perhaps the most profound transformations I've observed involve children affected by bullying. Both those who have been targeted and those who might have become bullies themselves.

Bullying remains one of the most pressing issues facing Australian children today. Statistics suggest that approximately one in four Australian students experience bullying, with consequences ranging from poor academic performance to anxiety, depression, and in tragic cases, self-harm. Parents desperately seek solutions, and many turn to martial arts hoping to help their children. However, there's often a misunderstanding about what martial arts offers children facing bullying situations.

Let's explore how traditional martial arts training—particularly styles like karate that emphasise character development alongside physical technique—addresses bullying from multiple angles. It's not simply about teaching children to defend themselves physically (though that's one component). More importantly, it's about building the internal qualities that make children less likely to be targeted, more capable of responding appropriately when they are, and crucially, less likely to become bullies themselves.

Before we talk about how martial arts helps, we must understand what we're addressing. Bullying isn't a simple childhood conflict. It's characterised by an imbalance of power, repetitive harmful behavior, and intent to cause distress. It manifests as physical aggression, verbal abuse, social exclusion, or increasingly, cyberbullying.

Children who are bullied often share certain characteristics: they may appear vulnerable, anxious, or physically weak; they might lack confidence or struggle to assert boundaries; they may be perceived as "different" in some way. Importantly, being bullied is never the child's fault, but understanding these patterns helps us recognise how martial arts training addresses underlying vulnerabilities.

Children who bully often have their own struggles. Research indicates many lack empathy, have poor emotional regulation, may have experienced aggression themselves, or lack positive role models for respectful behavior. They may feel powerless in other areas of life and attempt to gain power through dominating others.

Martial arts addresses both sides of this equation. Building resilience in potential targets whilst cultivating respect and empathy in all students, including those who might otherwise develop bullying tendencies.

The most immediate and visible change in children who begin martial arts training is the growth of confidence. This isn't the false bravado that might lead to aggressive behavior; it's a quiet, genuine self-assurance that comes from competence and self-knowledge.

Mastery builds confidence: When a child struggles to execute a proper front kick for weeks, then suddenly gets it right, something shifts internally. They've proven to themselves that persistence pays off, that they can improve, that they're capable. This achievement is entirely their own—no one can do a kata for them or execute their techniques. The confidence that develops from genuine accomplishment is unshakeable.

Physical capability matters: Let's be honest—knowing you're physically capable, that you could defend yourself if absolutely necessary, changes how you carry yourself. Children who train in martial arts develop better posture, stronger body language, and move with more certainty. Bullies instinctively seek out targets who appear vulnerable. A child who walks with confidence, makes eye contact, and occupies space with assurance is simply less likely to be selected as a target.

However, and this is crucial—we never teach children that physical response is the first, or even second, solution to bullying. Physical self-defence is the last resort, used only when in immediate physical danger and escape isn't possible. The confidence martial arts builds is primarily about internal strength and self-respect, not fighting prowess.

Voice and boundary setting: In our dojo, we regularly practice the verbal components of self-defence—speaking firmly, saying "no" clearly, using assertive body language. Many children who are bullied struggle to assert boundaries. They may freeze, look down, or speak softly when confronted. Karate training, with its emphasis on the kiai (shout) and strong, direct communication, helps children find their voice.

I've had many parents tell me that their child's changed demeanour alone: walking taller, speaking more confidently, making eye contact—led to bullying stopping without any physical confrontation whatsoever. Bullies rarely persist with targets who clearly won't accept mistreatment.

The Awareness and Safety Skills
Martial arts training develops heightened awareness that serves children in multiple ways. Situational awareness: We teach students to be aware of their surroundings, to notice who's around them, to identify potential problems before they escalate. This isn't about paranoia; it's about being present and observant. A child who's paying attention can avoid many bullying situations entirely by choosing different routes, staying near adults or friends, or leaving situations that feel unsafe.

Reading body language: Through partner work and sparring practice, students become skilled at reading non-verbal cues. Children learn to recognise when someone is agitated, aggressive, or potentially threatening. This skill helps them navigate social situations more effectively and respond appropriately to warning signs.

De-escalation strategies: Traditional martial arts philosophies emphasise avoiding conflict whenever possible. We explicitly teach children that walking away from confrontation isn't cowardice—it's wisdom. We role-play scenarios where children practice:
- Using calm, non-confrontational language
- Removing themselves from situations before they escalate
- Seeking adult help appropriately
- Recognising when a situation requires immediate intervention from authorities

Physical awareness: Children who train in martial arts develop body awareness and control that translates to daily life. They're less likely to accidentally invade others' personal space, more aware of appropriate physical boundaries, and better able to recognise when their own boundaries are being violated.

The Respect Culture: The Heart of the Solution
Here's where we reach the core of how martial arts addresses bullying from both sides. Traditional martial arts dojos are, fundamentally, communities built on respect.

What We Mean by Respect
In the dojo, respect isn't just politeness. It's a comprehensive approach to how we interact with others and ourselves.

Respect for instructors and seniors: Students bow to instructors, address them properly, and listen attentively. This isn't about authoritarian control; it's about acknowledging the knowledge and experience others offer us.

Respect for peers: Students of all abilities train together. The advanced student helps the beginner. The strong support the weak. The quick assist the slow. We explicitly teach that everyone's journey is different, and we celebrate each person's progress rather than comparing or competing destructively.

Respect for oneself: Perhaps most importantly, we teach self-respect. This means caring for your body, pushing your limits appropriately, acknowledging your achievements, and treating yourself with the same kindness you'd show others.

Respect for the art: Students care for their uniform, maintain the dojo space, and approach training with sincerity and effort. These practices cultivate a general attitude of care and respect that extends beyond the dojo.

How Respect Prevents Bullying Behaviour
Children who genuinely understand and embody respect do not bully others. Let me explain why:

Empathy development: The respect we teach includes recognition that others have feelings, struggles, and value. When you've bowed to your training partner, worked together on techniques, helped them improve, and received their help in return, you can't easily objectify or harm them. Partner training in martial arts builds empathy in a visceral, physical way.

When children practice controlled sparring, they learn directly what it feels like to be hit, even lightly. They understand the vulnerability of allowing someone close to you in combat scenarios. This builds a deep understanding of others' vulnerability that translates to compassion outside the dojo.

Image by Luidmila Chernetska

Power and responsibility: Martial arts students are repeatedly taught that with physical capability comes responsibility. We emphasise that techniques are for self-defence only, never for aggression or showing off. Students who violate this principle face serious consequences, including dismissal from the dojo.

I tell my students: The strongest martial artist is the one who never needs to fight. This message—that true strength is shown through restraint, kindness, and protecting others—is antithetical to bullying behavior.

Self-regulation: Martial arts training is challenging. Students face frustration, failure, and discomfort regularly. Through this, they develop emotional regulation and stress management skills. Children who can manage their own emotions don't lash out at others to feel powerful.

Positive outlet: Children who might have aggressive tendencies or excess energy find an appropriate outlet in martial arts. The physical intensity of training, combined with the disciplined structure, channels energy constructively rather than destructively.

Positive identity: Being a martial artist becomes part of a child's identity—and it's an identity built on positive values. Children think, "I'm a karateka, and karateka don't bully people." This internal identity becomes a guide for behavior.

The Dojo as Safe Community

For children who've been bullied or feel socially isolated, the dojo offers something precious: belonging.

Acceptance: In our dojo, what matters is effort, respect, and character—not social status, physical appearance, academic achievement, or any of the other factors by which children are often judged. The child who's targeted at school for being "different" finds acceptance in the dojo.

Positive peer relationships: Children train alongside others who share their interest in martial arts. Friendships formed in the dojo often become some of children's strongest relationships, providing social support that extends beyond training.

Adult mentorship: Quality martial arts instructors serve as positive role models, offering guidance, encouragement, and sometimes simply a listening ear. For children lacking positive adult influences, this relationship can be transformative.

Earned achievement: In a world where children sometimes feel powerless, martial arts offers a clear path to achievement. Belt progression is earned through genuine effort and skill development. No one can give it to you or take it away. This builds a sense of agency and control.

Practical Strategies Martial Arts Teaches

Beyond the psychological and social benefits, martial arts provides children with practical strategies for addressing bullying:

The assertive response: We practice responding to verbal aggression with calm, firm statements: "Stop. I don't like that." "That's not okay." "Leave me alone." These simple phrases, delivered with confident body language, are often enough to stop bullying behavior.

The broken record technique: If the bully persists, we teach children to repeat their statement calmly without engaging in argument or showing emotional reaction. Bullies seek a reaction; children who refuse to provide one become less interesting targets.

Strategic distance: We teach children to maintain appropriate physical distance from potential threats. If someone is being aggressive, you step back, creating space. This is both a physical safety strategy and a non-escalatory response.

Seeking help appropriately: We explicitly teach that telling adults about bullying isn't "snitching"—it's appropriate help-seeking. We distinguish between tattling (trying to get someone in trouble for minor issues) and reporting (seeking help for serious, harmful behavior).

Documentation: For persistent bullying, we encourage children and parents to document incidents—dates, times, what happened, who witnessed it. This information is crucial when involving school authorities.

When Physical Self-Defence is Appropriate
We must address this directly: there are situations where physical self-defence may be necessary.

If a child is in immediate physical danger—being hit, grabbed, or physically attacked—they have the right to defend themselves. Martial arts training provides the skills to do so effectively and proportionally.

However, we teach clear guidelines:

Use minimum necessary force: The goal is to create an opportunity to escape, not to "win a fight" or inflict harm.

Defend, don't attack: Martial arts techniques are never for initiating aggression.

Escape is the priority: Even if you could physically dominate the situation, the wisest choice is to get to safety and adult help.

Report immediately: Any physical altercation must be reported to parents and school authorities, even if the child successfully defended themselves.

I've taught karate to hundreds of children, and very few have ever needed to use physical self-defence against bullying. The vast majority find that the confidence, awareness, and verbal skills they've developed prevent situations from escalating to physical confrontation.

The Role of Parents and Instructors
Addressing bullying requires partnership between martial arts training, parents, and schools.

Parents must:
- Maintain open communication with children about their social experiences
- Take reports of bullying seriously and investigate appropriately
- Work with schools to address bullying behavior
- Reinforce the values taught in the dojo
- Model respectful behavior in their own interactions
- Understand that martial arts is one component of addressing bullying, not a complete solution

Instructors must:
- Create genuinely respectful, inclusive dojo environments
- Actively teach anti-bullying values alongside physical techniques
- Address any bullying behavior within the dojo immediately and seriously
- Communicate with parents about children's development and any concerns
- Provide age-appropriate reality-based training while maintaining safety
- Recognise signs that children may be struggling and offer support

Schools must:
- Take bullying reports seriously and investigate thoroughly
- Implement evidence-based anti-bullying programs
- Create safe reporting mechanisms for students
- Apply appropriate consequences for bullying behavior
- Support targeted students without stigmatising them
- Recognise that martial arts training is legitimate skill development, not promotion of violence

Real Transformation: Stories from the Dojo

Over the years, I've witnessed remarkable transformations.

The quiet eight-year-old who was daily targeted with verbal abuse and social exclusion. After six months of training, she walked differently, spoke up in class, and made friends in the dojo. The bullying gradually stopped—not because she fought back, but because she no longer presented as an easy target.

The physically large twelve-year-old boy who was using his size to intimidate smaller children at school. His parents enrolled him in our dojo hoping to "channel his energy." What actually happened was more profound: through learning to control his power in sparring, receiving correction when he was too rough, and being held to high behavioural standards, he developed restraint and empathy. He became a protective presence for smaller students rather than a threatening one.

The ten-year-old who had been physically bullied and was terrified. Karate didn't make him capable of fighting off his bullies (though he did develop skills). What it did was build his confidence enough that he could clearly tell adults what was happening, and his changed demeanour meant he was no longer targeted once the school addressed the situation.

These cases are representative of what happens when children are immersed in a culture of respect, capability, and mutual support.

The Bigger Picture: Creating Respectful Humans

Ultimately, the relationship between martial arts and bullying is about something larger than individual incidents. It's about creating human beings who fundamentally respect others.

A child who has learned genuine respect—who understands that everyone deserves dignity, who recognises others' vulnerability, who uses power responsibly, who stands up for the weak—is not only unlikely to bully but likely to be part of the solution. These children become the ones who befriend isolated classmates, who speak up when they witness mistreatment, who create inclusive environments.

Conversely, a child who has learned self-respect, who knows their own worth, who possesses genuine confidence and capability—this child is resilient against attempts to diminish them.

Martial arts doesn't "fix" bullying. Bullying is a complex social issue requiring comprehensive approaches including school policies, parental involvement, social-emotional education, and sometimes professional mental health support. But martial arts can be a powerful component of the solution, addressing root causes rather than just symptoms.

A Path Forward

If your child is facing bullying, or if you're concerned they might be developing bullying behaviours, consider what quality martial arts training offers: a community built on respect, a path to genuine confidence, practical skills for navigating social challenges, positive peer relationships, adult mentorship, and most importantly, a framework for understanding their own worth and the worth of others.

Look for schools that emphasise traditional values alongside physical techniques, that maintain high behavioural standards, that create inclusive environments, and where instructors genuinely care about students' character development, not just their competitive success. The techniques children learn in martial arts are useful. The confidence they develop is valuable. But the respect they embody—for themselves and others—is transformative. It changes not just how they respond to bullying, but who they become as human beings.

And perhaps that's the most important lesson: we don't just teach children to defend against bullies. We teach them to become the kind of people who make bullying less likely to occur in the first place. That's the true power of martial arts.

Author Don McKay is a 5th Dan teaching Kofukan Karate at his Karate For Life dojos in Perth's southern suburbs. For more information see: https://www.karateforlife.net

Image by Lady Designer

FROM THE GROUND UP

32

Essential Foot Care for Martial Artists
by Amy Lynch

We spend considerable time perfecting our hand techniques, refining our stances, and developing our mental discipline. Yet how often do we give proper attention to the foundation of all our training—our feet? Whether you're a karateka executing powerful mae-geri, a taekwondo practitioner flying through the air, or a judoka maintaining balance during throws, your feet are fundamental to everything you do. They deserve respect, care, and attention that matches their importance.

I've witnessed every foot-related issue imaginable: from minor blisters that interrupt training to serious fractures that sideline students for months. I've also observed that practitioners who invest in proper foot care not only avoid many common injuries but also perform better and train more consistently. This article addresses both the unglamorous but essential topic of foot hygiene and grooming, and the more dramatic reality of managing common foot injuries.

The Foundation: Understanding Your Feet

Before we discuss care and injury management, let's appreciate what remarkable structures our feet are. Each foot contains 26 bones, 33 joints, and more than 100 muscles, tendons, and ligaments. This complex architecture allows for the incredible range of movement martial arts demands—from the explosive push-off in a jumping kick to the subtle weight shifts in kata, from absorbing the impact of landing to maintaining balance on one leg.

In many martial arts, particularly traditional styles like karate, kung fu, and taekwondo, we train barefoot. This direct connection to the ground develops proprioception (awareness of body position), strengthens the intrinsic foot muscles, and maintains the tactile sensitivity that helps us feel our connection to the earth. However, barefoot training also exposes our feet to unique challenges that require proactive care

Hygiene: The Non-Negotiable Foundation
Let's address the topic many martial artists would rather avoid but every dojo member must embrace: foot hygiene. Training barefoot in a shared space creates an environment where fungi, bacteria, and viruses can spread if we're not diligent. Beyond preventing personal discomfort and infection, maintaining excellent foot hygiene is a matter of respect—for yourself, your training partners, and your dojo.
Daily Hygiene Practices

Washing: This seems obvious, yet it bears stating explicitly. Wash your feet daily with soap and warm water, paying particular attention to the spaces between your toes where moisture and bacteria accumulate. If you've trained that day, wash your feet immediately after class, not hours later when you finally get home. Many dojos provide washing facilities specifically for this purpose—use them.

Keep a small towel in your training bag specifically for drying your feet thoroughly after washing. Fungi thrive in warm, moist environments, so ensuring your feet are completely dry, especially between the toes, is crucial. Don't just wave your feet in the air and call them dry—actually towel them properly.

Nail care: Keep your toenails trimmed short and filed smooth. Long toenails are weapons waiting to injure your training partners during kicks or grappling. They also provide hiding places for bacteria and fungus. Cut nails straight across to prevent ingrown toenails (a painful condition that can stop you training), then file any sharp edges. Do this regularly—nail care isn't a once-monthly activity.

Inspection: Develop the habit of examining your feet daily. Look for cuts, blisters, areas of redness or swelling, changes in skin texture, or anything unusual. Early detection of problems allows for early treatment before minor issues become major ones.

Preventing Fungal Infections
Athlete's foot (tinea pedis) is the bane of many martial artists' existence. This fungal infection causes itching, burning, cracking, and peeling skin, typically between the toes or on the soles of the feet. Prevention is far easier than treatment:

Keep feet dry: Change out of sweaty socks promptly after training. If your feet sweat heavily, consider using antifungal powder in your daily footwear.

Avoid walking barefoot in communal areas: Wear thongs (flip-flops) in changing rooms, showers, and around pools. The dojo training floor should be the only place your bare feet touch.

Don't share towels or footwear: This should be obvious, but it's worth stating.

Air out training gear: If you use foot guards or any foot-related protective equipment, ensure they dry completely between uses.

Treat promptly: If you notice signs of athlete's foot, treat it immediately with over-the-counter antifungal cream and continue treatment for the full recommended duration, even after symptoms disappear. If it doesn't improve within a week or worsens, see a healthcare professional.

Wart Prevention and Management
Plantar warts (verrucas) are viral infections that appear as small, rough growths on the soles of the feet. They're contagious and can be picked up from contaminated surfaces in gyms and changing rooms.

Prevention involves the same principles as fungal infection prevention—wearing protective footwear in communal areas and maintaining good hygiene. If you develop a plantar wart, cover it with a waterproof dressing during training to prevent spreading it to others, and seek treatment. Over-the-counter treatments can work, but stubborn warts may require professional treatment from a podiatrist.

Dojo Hygiene Responsibilities
As practitioners, we share responsibility for dojo cleanliness:
- Ensure your feet are clean before stepping onto the training floor
- Never train with open wounds on your feet unless they're properly covered with waterproof dressings
- If you have a fungal infection or wart, inform your instructor and take appropriate precautions
- Support dojo cleaning and maintenance efforts

"The path is always right beneath your feet."

Issan Dorsey

Image by Aflo

Grooming and Conditioning

Beyond basic hygiene, proper grooming and conditioning prepare your feet for the demands of martial arts training.

Callus Management

Barefoot training naturally develops calluses on the balls of the feet, heels, and sometimes the edges of the feet. Some callus development is beneficial—it provides natural protection. However, excessive callusing can become problematic, as very thick calluses can crack and become painful or infected.

The key is balance. Use a pumice stone or foot file regularly (on slightly dampened skin after bathing) to keep calluses from becoming too thick. File gently—you're not trying to remove all the callused skin, just preventing excessive build-up. Follow with moisturiser to keep the skin supple.

Moisturising

Dry, cracked skin on the feet isn't just unsightly—it creates entry points for infection and can be painful. Apply a good quality foot cream or moisturiser daily, particularly to the heels. Do this before bed, allowing the moisturiser to absorb overnight. In particularly dry climates (like much of Australia), you might need to moisturise daily.

However, don't moisturise immediately before training, slippery feet on the dojo floor are dangerous. Morning moisturising is fine if you train in the evening; evening moisturising works if you train in the morning.

Flexibility and Strength

Healthy feet aren't just clean feet—they're strong, flexible feet. Incorporate foot-specific exercises into your routine:

Toe exercises: Practice picking up small objects (marbles, pencils) with your toes to strengthen the intrinsic foot muscles.

Ankle rotations: Rotate your ankles through their full range of motion daily to maintain flexibility.

Toe spreading: Practice spreading your toes apart and holding the position. This strengthens the small muscles and improves balance.

Balance work: Standing on one foot, particularly on slightly unstable surfaces, strengthens the entire foot and ankle complex.

These exercises take just a few minutes daily but contribute significantly to foot health and martial arts performance.

Common Foot Injuries

Despite our best preventive efforts, injuries happen. Understanding common foot injuries helps you respond appropriately.

Bruising and Contusions

Bruising is perhaps the most common foot injury in martial arts. It occurs when impact causes small blood vessels to break, leading to discolouration, tenderness, and swelling. Common causes include landing incorrectly from jumps, impact during kicking practice, or stepping on equipment.

Immediate treatment (RICE protocol):

- Rest: Stop the activity that caused the injury
- Ice: Apply ice wrapped in a thin towel for 15-20 minutes every 2-3 hours for the first 48 hours
- Compression: Use an elastic bandage if swelling is significant, but not so tight it cuts off circulation
- Elevation: Keep the foot raised above heart level when possible

Recovery expectations: Minor bruising typically resolves within 1-2 weeks. During this time, you may be able to continue modified training that doesn't stress the injured area. Severe bruising may require several weeks off from activities that impact the affected area.

Warning signs: If bruising is accompanied by significant swelling, inability to bear weight, severe pain, or doesn't improve within a week, seek medical evaluation to rule out fracture.

Blisters

Blisters form when friction causes the skin layers to separate and fluid to accumulate. In martial arts, they commonly occur on the balls of the feet from pivoting, on the toes from kicking, or on the heels from footwork drills.

Prevention:
- Gradually increase training intensity to allow skin to toughen
- Ensure proper technique (incorrect pivoting often causes excessive friction)
- Keep feet dry during training
- Address hot spots immediately (areas of redness or tenderness) by applying protective padding before blisters form

Treatment of intact blisters: If the blister is small and intact, leave it alone—the skin provides natural protection. Cover with a protective plaster if it's in an area that will receive continued friction. Avoid training on that specific area until it heals.

Treatment of broken blisters: Clean thoroughly with soap and water, apply antiseptic, and cover with a sterile dressing. Change the dressing daily and watch for signs of infection (increased redness, warmth, pus, red streaks). If a blister becomes infected, see a healthcare professional.

Sprains and Strains

Ankle sprains are incredibly common in martial arts, occurring when ligaments are stretched or torn, typically by rolling the ankle inward or outward. Strains involve muscles or tendons rather than ligaments.

Severity grades:
- Grade 1: Mild stretching with minimal tearing, minimal swelling, minor pain
- Grade 2: Partial tearing, moderate swelling and pain, some instability
- Grade 3: Complete tear, severe swelling and pain, significant instability

Immediate treatment: RICE protocol as described above. For grades 2 and 3, seek medical evaluation.

Recovery and rehabilitation: This is crucial. Many martial artists make the mistake of returning to training too soon, leading to chronic ankle instability and repeated injuries. Follow your healthcare provider's rehabilitation protocol, which typically includes:

- Range of motion exercises
- Strengthening exercises
- Proprioception training (balance work)
- Gradual return to martial arts activities

Even after you feel better, continue ankle strengthening exercises indefinitely to prevent reinjury.

Fractures

Broken bones in the feet are serious injuries requiring proper medical treatment. They can occur from direct impact, landing incorrectly, or from stress (stress fractures develop gradually from repetitive impact).

Common fracture sites in martial artists:
- Metatarsals (long bones of the foot)
- Toes (particularly the fifth toe from impact injuries)
- Calcaneus (heel bone)

Suspect a fracture if you experience:
- Immediate, severe pain at the time of injury
- Inability to bear weight
- Significant swelling
- Visible deformity
- Severe bruising
- A snapping or popping sound at the time of injury

Action required: Stop training immediately and seek medical attention. Do not attempt to "walk it off." X-rays or other imaging will confirm the diagnosis.

Recovery expectations: Fracture healing typically requires 6-8 weeks minimum, though this varies based on the specific bone, fracture severity, and individual factors. Follow your doctor's instructions precisely regarding weight-bearing restrictions and activity modifications.

Stress fractures: These develop gradually from repetitive impact and may present as persistent pain that worsens with activity and improves with rest. They're particularly common in the metatarsals. If you have persistent foot pain that doesn't resolve with a few days' rest, seek evaluation. Stress fractures require rest and modification of training to prevent progression to complete fractures.

Plantar Fasciitis

This overuse injury involves inflammation of the plantar fascia, the thick band of tissue running along the bottom of the foot from heel to toes. It's common in martial artists due to the repetitive impact and stress on the feet.

Symptoms:
- Sharp pain in the heel or arch, particularly with the first steps in the morning
- Pain that improves with movement but worsens after long periods on your feet
- Pain after (not usually during) training

Treatment:
- Rest from high-impact activities
- Ice massage (freeze water in a paper cup, peel back the cup, and massage the affected area)
- Stretching exercises for the calf and plantar fascia

- Strengthening exercises for the foot muscles
- Proper footwear support when not training
- Night splints (in chronic cases)
- Professional treatment if self-care doesn't improve symptoms within several weeks

Prevention: Maintain calf and foot flexibility, strengthen foot muscles, avoid rapid increases in training intensity, and address biomechanical issues (such as overpronation) with appropriate footwear or orthotics for daily wear.

Sesamoiditis

The sesamoids are two small bones embedded in the tendon under the big toe joint. Sesamoiditis is inflammation of these bones and surrounding tissues, common in martial artists who spend lots of time on the balls of the feet.

Symptoms:
- Pain under the big toe, particularly when pushing off
- Tenderness when pressing on the ball of the foot
- Pain that worsens with barefoot activity

Management:
- Rest from activities that stress the area
- Ice application
- Padding to relieve pressure on the affected area
- Modified training that minimises pushing off from the affected foot
- Professional evaluation if symptoms persist

Return to Training: A Gradual Process

One of the most difficult aspects of injury management for dedicated martial artists is patience during recovery. The eagerness to return to training often leads to premature return and reinjury.

Follow these principles:

Obtain clearance: For significant injuries, get medical clearance before returning to training.

Start gradually: Don't resume at your pre-injury intensity. Begin with basic techniques, reduced duration, and lower intensity.

Listen to your body: Some discomfort during rehabilitation is normal, but sharp pain or swelling indicates you're pushing too hard.

Modify as needed: You may be able to train upper body techniques while a foot injury heals, or practice kata at reduced intensity.

Build progressively: Gradually increase training volume and intensity over several weeks.

Continue rehabilitation exercises: Even after returning to training, continue strengthening and flexibility work for the injured area.

Prevention: Your Best Strategy

While we've covered treatment extensively, prevention deserves equal emphasis:

Proper warm-up: Always warm up thoroughly, including specific ankle and foot mobilisation.

Technique over power: Especially when learning new techniques, prioritise proper form over force or speed.

Appropriate progression: Don't attempt advanced techniques before you've mastered the fundamentals.

Quality training surface: Train on appropriate surfaces that provide some shock absorption. Concrete or extremely hard floors increase injury risk.

Conditioning: Regular conditioning of the feet through progressive barefoot training strengthens the structures and prepares them for martial arts demands.

Cross-training: Activities like swimming provide cardiovascular benefits without foot impact, allowing recovery time.

Rest: Include rest days in your training schedule. Overtraining is a primary contributor to overuse injuries.

When to Seek Professional Help

Consult a healthcare professional (GP, physiotherapist, or podiatrist) if you experience:
- Severe pain that doesn't improve with rest and basic care
- Inability to bear weight
- Visible deformity
- Significant swelling that doesn't reduce with RICE protocol
- Signs of infection (increasing redness, warmth, pus, red streaks, fever)
- Numbness or tingling
- Persistent pain that interferes with daily activities
- Recurring injuries in the same location

Don't let pride or impatience prevent you from seeking appropriate care. Early professional intervention often prevents minor issues from becoming major, chronic problems.

Respect From the Ground Up

In Japanese martial arts, there's a saying: "The beginning is at the feet." This holds true both technically and practically. Our feet carry us through every technique, every kata, every training session. They connect us to the earth and provide the foundation for everything we do in martial arts.

Caring for your feet—through diligent hygiene, thoughtful grooming, appropriate injury management, and preventive strategies—isn't vanity or weakness. It's fundamental wisdom. It's respecting the tools that allow you to pursue your martial arts journey. It's honouring the body that serves you so faithfully.

The most successful martial artists I've known aren't necessarily those with the most natural talent or the most powerful techniques. They're the ones who train consistently over years and decades, and consistency requires staying healthy. That begins with taking care of your foundation—your feet.

Invest the time in daily foot care. Be patient with injuries. Seek help when needed. Your feet will carry you far in your martial arts journey if you treat them with the respect they deserve.

Women in Martial Arts Workshop 2025
Empowering Women Through Martial Arts

by Ann Draper

Women's participation in martial arts has experienced remarkable growth globally. Female practitioners now represent approximately 30% of all martial arts participants, up from 20% just a decade ago. This surge reflects greater emphasis on self-defense training, the growing popularity of female role models in martial arts, and the expansion of women-friendly training facilities. Karate and taekwondo show the highest female participation rates, with approximately 31% and 35% of total memberships respectively being female. Research indicates that women who practice martial arts are 25% more likely to report increased self-esteem, demonstrating the profound personal impact beyond physical skills.

Despite this progress, only 20.7% of martial arts instructors are female, highlighting the continued need for events that celebrate and support women's leadership in the martial arts community.

Celebrating Women in Action: October 18, 2025

On Saturday, 18th October 2025, female martial arts enthusiasts in Western Australia gathered for an unforgettable Women In Martial Arts workshop, contributing to this global movement and celebrating the strength and diversity of women in the industry.

The event featured an action-packed 4-hour session with instructors from three styles of Karate, plus Brazilian Jiu Jitsu, Boxing, and Bo (Staff).

Karate: Building Strength and Focus
The day kicked off with two high-energy Karate sessions led by Kim Benn (KUA Australia) and Tabitha Ingle (GKR Karate). Through a series of drills and techniques emphasizing proper form, participants developed strength, agility, and mental focus while tapping into their inner confidence.

Brazilian Jiu Jitsu and Boxing: Dynamic Skills and Techniques

Johanna Skiba led the Brazilian Jiu Jitsu session, focusing on ground control and submission techniques using the guillotine choke. The class emphasised dynamic movements, transitions, and the importance of safety, respect, and good sportsmanship on the mat.

Meg Croucher's Boxing session covered foundational skills including proper stance, footwork, balance, and agile movement for evading punches and creating counterattack opportunities. Participants learned various punches (jab, cross, hooks, and uppercuts) and defensive techniques (slipping, bobbing, and blocking) through drills with hand pads and partner work, all while emphasizing proper technique and safety.

Bo (Staff): Traditional Weapon Arts
The final session was led by seasoned Goju Ryu practitioner and event organizer Ann Draper. This unique opportunity introduced participants to traditional Okinawan Bo staff techniques, including:
- Grip and staff handling techniques
- Striking methods (overhead strikes, side strikes, thrusts, and sweeps)
- Footwork and body shifting

Partner drills (Bunkai) focusing on timing, coordination, distance, and spacing

A Celebration of Women in Martial Arts
The workshop provided a supportive environment for women from diverse backgrounds and martial arts disciplines to learn, grow, and connect with like-minded individuals. As one participant noted, "I've never felt so inspired and motivated to continue my martial arts journey."

By creating a platform for women to share knowledge, experiences, and mutual support, the event was a resounding success and a testament to the growing presence and influence of women in martial arts. Events like this contribute to building the next generation of female practitioners and instructors, helping to close the gender gap in martial arts leadership. We look forward to seeing the continued impact and growth of women in the martial arts community.

Women in Martial Arts
WORKSHOP

Contact Ann for more information

4-Hour Workshop
Open to All Styles*
LIMITED PLACES

REGISTER NOW!

Info for 2026 coming soon!

📍 GKR Karate Dojo - 1/17 Saltair Way, PORT KENNEDY

REQUIREMENTS*
Women must be 15+ y/o with a minimum 2 years Martial Arts experience
Equipment | Full Gi, Martial Arts attire, gloves, mouthguard and Bo (staff)

For more information CONTACT

 0417 992 019
 women.inmartialarts1@gmail.com

INSTRUCTORS
AnnDraper | GojuRyu Karate-Bo (Staff)
Kim Benn | KUA Karate
Tabitha Ingle | GKR Karate
Meg Croucher | Boxing "The Agoge"

Beyond the Bruise

Unlocking the Ancient Secrets of Dit Da Medicine

by Sifu David Richardson

Forget everything you think you know about treating an injury. In the world where martial arts mastery meets profound healing, there exists a sophisticated system that goes far beyond a simple rub or an ice pack. This is Dit Da Medicine, the warrior's art of recovery.

You've seen it in classic kung fu films: the old master pulls out a dark, mysterious bottle after a fierce battle, pouring a brown liquid onto his student's bruises. Or perhaps you've noticed a seasoned martial artist at your local gym with a distinctive black patch stuck to their shoulder or knee.

This isn't movie magic or a simple bandage. It's the visible tip of an iceberg—a complete and intricate medical philosophy born from the boxing halls of ancient China, known as Dit Da Jow (跌打酒) and Dit Da Medicine (跌打醫). Literally translated as "Fall and Strike Medicine," it is a holistic system for treating traumatic injury that has been refined over centuries. For a Western audience accustomed to R.I.C.E. (Rest, Ice, Compression, Elevation) and anti-inflammatory pills, understanding Dit Da offers a revolutionary perspective on how the body can heal.

At its core, Dit Da is fundamentally different from a Western-style sports massage or chiropractic adjustment. While those are excellent therapies for musculoskeletal alignment and relaxation, Dit Da is a targeted medical practice rooted in the principles of Traditional Chinese Medicine (TCM).

Dit Dat Dow - Herbal Relief Liniment

The central concept is "stagnation" specifically, blood stagnation (Yu Xue) and Qi (vital energy) stagnation. From a Dit Da perspective, a traumatic impact—a fall, a strike, a twist—disrupts and congests the normal flow of blood and energy in the affected area. This causes pain, swelling, bruising, and if left untreated, can lead to chronic weakness, stiffness, and a propensity for re-injury.

"Western medicine often focuses on suppressing the inflammatory response with ice and drugs like ibuprofen," explains Wing Chun Ling Tung Gong Master Dave Richardson. "We see inflammation as a part of the process, but we don't want it to stagnate. Our goal is to actively move it, to transform the stagnant blood and guide the body's own healing resources to the injury site. It's the difference between blocking a road and clearing a traffic jam."

冬季行脈圖

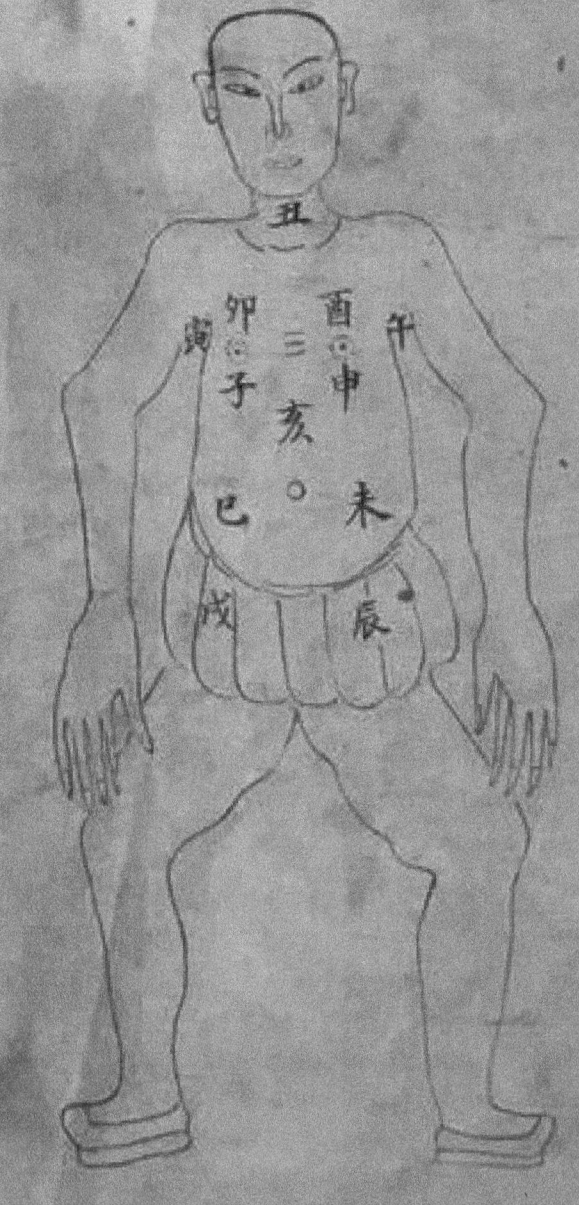

先師祕傳總訣

師曰：學武要害實訣，須知春夏秋冬四季分十二時辰方可以斷生死。若不大傷心之事不可行之，倘出外往別方或因路途險阻偶遇惡人，此手自不可忍，若非惡人何必傷人之命也。此手出在三尖何為三尖？虎尖、掌尖、眉尖，定要子午分明，百發百中。賢徒學習此手法，須傳師口訣，分明勢力工夫百中，難曉但使手須善而用之，若強妄不能成功矣。出手法須要虎尖、掌尖落眉尖落掌尖切

Stages of Warrior's Healing: A Dynamic Process

This philosophy dictates a multi-stage, timed approach, much like a skilled general deploying different strategies at different phases of a campaign. It's not a one-size-fits-all remedy, but a dynamic process.

Dit Da treatment is methodical. The wrong therapy at the wrong time can be counterproductive. Practitioners assess the injury and apply one or more of the primary treatment methods, each suited to a specific phase of healing.

The Herbal Compress (草藥熱敷 cou joek jit fu) & Herbal Plaster (膏藥 - gau joek)

In the first 24 to 72 hours after an injury, when the area is swollen, hot, and painful, the primary goal is to cool blood, reduce inflammation, stop pain, gently move blood by promoting circulation.

Modify the Jit Fu/Gao base formula by reducing or removing the very warm herbs like Hóng Huā, Táo Rén, Rǔ Xiāng, and Mò Yào.
Add cooling herbs for traumatic swelling, inflammation, and heat. To clear heat-toxin, invigorate blood and reduce inflammation.
This aromatic, warm compress is then applied directly to the injured area. Use the pack at a cool or lukewarm temperature, not hot.

The Western Parallel (and Divergence): This is where Dit Da most starkly contrasts with standard Western advice. We are told to apply ice. Dit Da applies warmth. Why? The logic is that cold causes contraction and constriction, potentially trapping inflammatory byproducts and slowing their removal. The herbal heat, however, aims to gently "open" the pores and superficial blood vessels, allowing the herbs to penetrate and the body to begin flushing out the metabolic waste of the injury. It's a proactive method of managing inflammation rather than suppressing it.

Dit Da Jow (跌打酒) & Therapeutic Manipulation

Once the initial, intense swelling has subsided, the focus shifts to breaking up deep bruising, realigning tissues, and restoring function.

The most famous tool of Dit Da: the Dit Da Jow liniment. "Jow" means "wine" or "liniment," and it is a potent blend of dozens of herbs like pseudoginseng (田七, Tián Qī), dragon's blood (血竭, Xuè Jié), and frankincense (乳香, Rǔ Xiāng) steeped in high-proof alcohol, which acts as a solvent and a carrier. The practitioner vigorously shakes the bottle, pours a small amount into their hand, and then applies it during a deep, focused massage.

The Manipulation Difference: This is not a relaxing, flowing Swedish massage. The techniques are often firm, targeted, and can be uncomfortable. The practitioner uses their fingers, knuckles, and even tools to work the Jow deep into the tendons, ligaments, and muscles. The dual purpose is to physically break apart adhesions and stubborn stagnation while driving the anti-inflammatory, circulation-enhancing, and bone-knitting herbs deep into the tissue. The Jow itself is a powerful medicine, with studies showing many of its key herbs have proven analgesic, anti-oedema, and anti-coagulant properties.

The Herbal Plaster (膏药 - Gāo Yào)

The final stage of healing is about consolidation, nourishment, and protection as the injury nears full recovery.

A thick, often pungent, herbal paste or a pre-made plaster can be applied directly to the skin over the injury site. These plasters, known as Dit Da Gao, contain herbs to strengthen tendons and bones, and others to nourish or move the blood. They are typically left on for 12 to 48 hours, providing a continuous, low-dose transdermal delivery of the herbal compounds.

The Modern Analogy: Think of this as a smart, time-release patch for musculoskeletal healing. While it protects the area like a standard brace, it actively works to nourish the deeper tissues, ensuring they heal strong and resilient, preventing the injury from becoming a chronic weak link.

Bridging the Worlds: Why Dit Da Matters Today

In an era of opioid crises and a growing understanding of the limitations of simply masking pain, systems like Dit Da offer a compelling, natural, and holistic alternative. It represents a paradigm where the body is not a machine to be fixed with isolated parts, but an integrated whole where energy, blood, and structure are inseparable.

"Western science is starting to catch up with what we've known for centuries," says Master Dave. "The research on herbs like turmeric (a cousin of some Dit Da ingredients) for inflammation, or the concept of fascia and its role in pain, all point toward the holistic principles Dit Da was built on."

For the modern athlete, the weekend warrior, or anyone dealing with the lingering effects of an old injury, the wisdom of Dit Da provides a powerful toolkit. It teaches us to see an injury not just as a damaged structure, but as a dynamic event in the body's landscape an event that can be navigated with intelligence, patience, and the profound power of plants.

So, the next time you see that dark plaster or smell the distinct, medicinal aroma of a Dit Da Jow bottle, you'll see beyond the mystery.

You'll see a sophisticated, time-tested science of healing, ready to help the body do what it does best: recover, adapt, and grow stronger.

Experience the difference of Dit Da Medicine for yourself.

Book a professional Dit Da treatment at our clinic to receive a personalized assessment and targeted therapy. For your own home practice, our high-quality Dit Da Jow, herbal plasters, and raw herbs are available for purchase. Begin your journey to deeper healing—contact us now to schedule your appointment or visit our online store.

www.kungfusouthside.com.au
www.lingtungtcmherbs.com.au

Email: sifu@kungfusouthside.com.au
Ph: (07) 38007007

Champions Made at Shaolin Kempo

by Maria Tan

After a 22-year hiatus, the Shaolin Kempo QLD tournament made a triumphant return to Brisbane, bringing together over 35 martial artists for a spectacular display of fighting artistry across three divisions and 13 categories. Held at the Mackenzie dojo, the 2025 tournament marked the first time Shaolin Kempo students had competed against each other since 2003, with participants demonstrating their skills in Wrestling, Chin Na, Push Hands, Katas, Weaponry and Sparring in Live Combat Self Defence.

Tournament Champions Crowned

The overall Tournament Champion Trophy was claimed by 21-year-old Cyma Joseph from Mackenzie, who also took home the adult division trophy. The Children's Tiger Trophy went to 11-year-old Rishaan Mehta from Mackenzie, while fellow Mackenzie student Juri Schmunk earned the Teen Dragons Trophy.

For Cyma Joseph, a green belt who has trained in Shaolin Kempo for five years, the victory was particularly meaningful. "It was positively overwhelming to win a tournament that hasn't been won in 22 years," she said.

"I love the competitive atmosphere in tournaments and getting to showcase new skills while seeing other students improve," Cyma explained, adding that she believes "Kempo is the best base to begin your journey in martial arts," due to its adaptability and support for specialisation in training.

The Shaolin Kempo System

Shaolin Kempo combines the circular, fluid motion of Chinese Kung Fu with the linear, powerful movements of Japanese Kenpo Karate, while also teaching Chen Style Tai Chi and Kempo Jitsu—a form incorporating elements of judo, wrestling and jiu jitsu that includes throws, sweeps, grappling, locks and chokes.

The system also emphasises weaponry training, including nun chucks, bow staff, tonfa, spears, twin sai, guandao, sticks and blades, providing students with a comprehensive martial arts education.

The Shaolin Kempo QLD school builds upon foundations laid by Ed Parker, founder of the American Kempo style, whose famous students included Bruce Lee, Chuck Norris, Steve McQueen and Elvis Presley.

5th Degree Black Belt Sifu Brendan Gray, emphasises the individualised approach to training at Shaolin Kempo QLD, "The training is designed specifically for each student at the pace at which they can retain information. We train differently nearly every night in a friendly atmosphere, and you don't get bored, as the class regularly switches things up between self-defence, grappling, weaponry and conditioning. I love helping others with their confidence, articulating control, balance and timing. I am so proud to watch each student's journey as they improve power, technique and coordination," he said.

Sifu Brendan Gray (left) and Di Sempai, Glen Pearson, children's Tiger's Trophy winner, Rishaan Mehta, teen Dragons Trophy winner, Juri Schmunk, and adult trophy winner Cyma Joseph.

SHAOLIN KEMPO
Martial Arts & Self Defence Training
https://shaolinkempoqld.com.au/

The tournament highlighted not just individual achievement, but the family-friendly nature of the school. Eleven-year-old white belt Rhys Tan-Inglis from Redland Bay, who has been training for three months, says he has learned more at Shaolin Kempo than in his previous three years of karate training.

"This is so much better than doing karate on its own. Shaolin Kempo blends so many different styles of martial arts into one and you learn so much more than you do at a regular martial arts school," Rhys said.

His mother, 43-year-old Maria Tan, switched to Shaolin Kempo specifically so she and her son could train together. "They even gave us a free bag after grading," Maria said. "I also get to do a meaningful activity with my son where we both learn new skills and I've managed to lose over 10kg while training at Shaolin Kempo without it even feeling like I was doing anything extreme."

Despite travelling from Redland Bay to Mackenzie to train during the week and on Saturdays, Maria says they are "loving every minute of it".

"This is the best thing we've ever done together and we're creating a stronger bond, lifelong memories, friendships and skills that we will carry with us for the rest of our lives. It is well worth the trip and truly puts the art into 'martial arts'."

Events like the Shaolin Kempo QLD tournament provide invaluable benefits to martial arts communities. Tournaments offer students the opportunity to test their skills in a controlled, supportive environment, building confidence and resilience while maintaining the respectful spirit of martial arts training.

For schools, tournaments strengthen community bonds, provide measurable goals for students, and showcase the effectiveness of their training methods. The 22-year gap since the last tournament made this year's event particularly special, bringing together multiple generations of practitioners and reigniting competitive spirit within the Shaolin Kempo QLD community.

Instructor and Di Sempai Glen Pearson reflects on the broader impact of martial arts: "Martial arts has had an enormous effect on most parts of my life, from giving me direction, coordination, fitness, confidence and the ability to learn many different moves and techniques, to having the discipline and grit to endure hard times in life."

Perhaps most significantly, the tournament exemplified martial arts' power to unite people from diverse backgrounds. Participants included students from India (Cyma Joseph, Rishaan Mehta), Germany (Juri Schmunk), China (Hamilton Lee), and Australia, with many students representing multiple cultural heritages, including Filipino, Chinese and Spanish ancestry.

In a world often marked by division, the Shaolin Kempo QLD tournament demonstrated that passion for martial arts transcends race, religion and political orientation, bringing people together in pursuit of excellence, discipline and mutual respect. The successful return of this tournament suggests a bright future for Shaolin Kempo QLD and provides a template for other martial arts schools seeking to build stronger communities through healthy competition.

Honouring Experience
Adapting Karate Training for Senior Practitioners
by Tony Johnston

As a karate instructor with many years of experience running traditional dojos, I've had the privilege of teaching students across every age group and ability level. Some of my most dedicated and inspiring students are those who have continued their karate journey well into their sixties, seventies, and beyond. These practitioners bring wisdom, discipline, and a depth of understanding to the dojo that enriches everyone around them. However, teaching senior students, particularly those managing arthritis, heart conditions, or other age-related health considerations, requires thoughtful adaptation without compromising the integrity of traditional karate training.

The challenge, and indeed the art, lies in modifying training dynamics whilst maintaining technical excellence. This isn't about lowering standards or creating a "watered-down" version of karate. It's about understanding that the essence of karate—precision, control, mindfulness, and the cultivation of character—can be pursued with equal dedication regardless of the speed or power with which techniques are delivered.

Understanding the Senior Practitioner
First, let's acknowledge an important truth: age is just one factor in determining a student's capabilities. I've taught sixty-five-year-olds who move with remarkable fluidity and eighty-year-olds with joint flexibility that would shame many younger students. Conversely, I've worked with relatively young practitioners dealing with significant physical limitations. The key is treating each student as an individual, not making assumptions based on birthdays.

That said, practitioners over sixty often face common challenges that we, as instructors, need to understand and respect:

Arthritis affects joints throughout the body, causing pain, stiffness, and reduced range of motion. The hands, knees, hips, and spine are commonly affected. Morning stiffness is typical, and weather changes can exacerbate symptoms. Cardiovascular considerations mean we must be mindful of heart rate, blood pressure, and recovery time. Many senior students are on medications that affect heart rate response to exercise.

Reduced bone density increases fracture risk, particularly in post-menopausal women. High-impact techniques require modification.

Balance and proprioception changes can affect stability, especially in complex stances or dynamic movements.

Recovery time extends with age. What might require one day's rest at thirty could need three days at seventy.

Medication effects can include dizziness, altered heart rate, or increased photosensitivity. Always encourage students to inform you of relevant health conditions and medications.

The Philosophy of Adaptation
Traditional karate, at its core, has always been about personal development rather than competition. This philosophical foundation makes it ideally suited for senior practitioners. The Japanese concept of "shuhari"—first learn the rules, then break the rules, then transcend the rules—applies beautifully to adapting training for older students.

Senior practitioners often possess deep technical knowledge. They understand why a technique works, the biomechanics behind it, and the strategic application. This understanding allows them to maintain technical precision even when physical dynamics must change. A perfectly executed slow-motion gyaku-zuki (reverse punch) with proper hip rotation, weight transfer, and body alignment demonstrates better karate than a fast, powerful punch with compromised technique.

I remind my instructors: we're not training these students to win tournaments. We're helping them maintain physical capability, mental acuity, social connection, and the sense of purpose that comes from continuous learning. That's worth infinitely more than explosive speed.

Adapting Kata: Maintaining Essence While Modifying Dynamics

Kata is the heart of traditional karate and, fortunately, one of the most adaptable training methods for senior practitioners. The solo nature of kata allows each student to work at their own pace whilst maintaining proper form and technique.

Speed Modifications
The concept of kata performed at different speeds isn't new—it's a legitimate training method used by practitioners of all ages. Slow kata practice, often called "yukkuri" or "take it slow" training, develops different skills than fast kata.

Slow kata enhances:
- Precise muscle control and body awareness
- Balance and stability in transitions
- Understanding of weight transfer and hip rotation
- Breath control and coordination
- Mindfulness and meditation through movement

For senior students, I recommend starting each kata slowly, focusing on absolute technical precision. Each stance must be correct, every hand position exact, all transitional movements smooth and controlled. This isn't "easier"—it's actually more demanding in terms of control, balance, and concentration.

As students warm up and feel comfortable, they can gradually increase speed in sections where they feel capable, always prioritising technique over velocity. Some students might perform the entire kata slowly; others might execute certain sequences with speed whilst moderating others. Both approaches are valid.

Power Modifications
Power in karate comes from proper technique, not muscular force. This is fantastic news for senior practitioners because it means they can generate effective techniques without the joint stress that comes from trying to muscle through movements.

Focus on:

Kime (focus) through technique rather than raw power. A punch that demonstrates proper hip rotation, body alignment, and timing exhibits kime even without tremendous force.

Controlled tension at the moment of impact rather than sustained tension throughout the movement. This reduces joint stress whilst maintaining the essential feeling of a focused technique.

Breath power (kiai) which engages the core and coordinates the entire body without requiring explosive muscular contraction.

Strategic chambering that demonstrates understanding of energy generation without necessarily unleashing full power.

I often tell my students: "Show me you could generate power with perfect technique, even if you choose not to fully release it." This maintains the spirit of the technique whilst protecting joints and cardiovascular system.

Stance Modifications for Joint Health

Stances are fundamental to karate, but they're also where many senior practitioners encounter difficulty, particularly those with knee or hip arthritis.

Zenkutsu-dachi (Forward Stance)
The traditional deep forward stance can be problematic for arthritic knees. Modifications include:
- Reducing the depth whilst maintaining correct weight distribution (70% front, 30% back)
- Ensuring the front knee tracks over the foot, never collapsing inward
- Allowing a slightly narrower width if hip flexibility is limited
- Focusing on the feeling of pushing the back leg forward rather than sinking deeply

Kiba-dachi (Horse Stance)
This side-facing stance can be particularly challenging. Adaptations include:
- Higher stance height, perhaps 30-40 degrees knee bend rather than deeper angles
- Maintaining proper knee alignment over feet
- Using a wall or barre for support during extended holds
- Emphasising the isometric engagement rather than the depth

Kokutsu-dachi (Back Stance)
This often suits senior practitioners well as it's naturally higher, but considerations include:
- Ensuring proper weight distribution without over-stressing the back knee
- Maintaining hip alignment without forcing rotation if hip flexibility is limited
- Using the stance's inherent stability to develop confidence

The crucial principle: stances must maintain their essential character—weight distribution, hip orientation, structural alignment—but depth and duration can be modified based on individual capability.

Modifying Striking Techniques
Punches, strikes, and blocks can be adapted whilst maintaining technical excellence.

Upper Body Techniques

For students with shoulder arthritis or rotator cuff issues:

- Full extension punches without hyperextension or locking the elbow
- Controlled chambering that doesn't force the shoulder into uncomfortable ranges
- Age-uke (rising block) with modified height if full overhead positions cause pain
- Emphasis on body rotation generating power rather than arm strength

For wrist or hand arthritis:

- Makiwara training is generally unsuitable; use focus pads with controlled contact
- Seiken (forefist) formation without forcing a tight fist if finger joints are painful
- Open-hand techniques (shuto, haito) as alternatives when appropriate
- Precision rather than power in all hand techniques

Lower Body Techniques

Kicks require particular attention for senior practitioners:

Mae-geri (Front Kick)

- Lower target height—waist level rather than head level
- Controlled extension without snapping or hyperextending the knee
- Using a wall or partner for balance if needed
- Slow, controlled practice to develop balance and hip flexibility

Mawashi-geri (Roundhouse Kick)

- Lower height with focus on hip rotation and pivot
- Modified chamber if hip flexibility limits the traditional high chamber
- Support available for balance during practice

Yoko-geri (Side Kick)

- Lower target with emphasis on proper hip positioning
- Controlled extension focusing on technique
- May substitute with yoko-geri-keage (side snap kick) at lower height

Many senior practitioners find that maintaining kicking ability, even at modified heights and speeds, significantly contributes to balance, flexibility, and functional independence in daily life.

Kumite Considerations

Partner work requires special attention with senior students.

Yakusoku Kumite (Prearranged Sparring)

This is ideal for older practitioners as it's controlled, predictable, and focuses on technique rather than speed or power:

- Clear communication between partners
- Controlled speed allowing both partners to execute techniques properly
- Focus on distance, timing, and technical precision

Opportunity to practice application without risk

Jiyu Kumite (Free Sparring)

Free sparring requires careful consideration:

- Non-contact or extremely controlled light contact only
- Protective equipment mandatory
- Emphasis on movement, distancing, and timing rather than power
- Shorter rounds with adequate rest
-

- Careful partner matching
- Understanding that many senior students may choose not to participate in jiyu kumite, and this is entirely acceptable

Class Structure for Mixed-Age Groups

Many dojos train students of various ages together. This presents both challenges and opportunities:

Warm-Up Modifications
- Longer, gentler warm-up for senior students
- Emphasis on joint mobilisation rather than dynamic stretching
- Individual pace for conditioning exercises
- Alternative exercises available (e.g., modified push-ups from knees or against wall)

Main Training
- Clear demonstration of modified versions alongside standard versions
- Senior students demonstrating precise, controlled technique whilst younger students show speed and power
- Partner pairing that respects both age and experience level
- Senior practitioners often make excellent mentors for technical precision

Cool-Down
- Extended cool-down period
- Gentle stretching within comfortable range of motion
- Emphasis on recovery and breathing

The Medical Conversation

Encourage senior students to:
- Obtain medical clearance before beginning or resuming training
- Inform instructors of relevant health conditions and medications
- Communicate immediately if they experience pain, dizziness, chest discomfort, or unusual symptoms
- Understand their exercise limitations (e.g., target heart rate ranges)
- Stay hydrated and take breaks as needed

As instructors, we're not medical professionals, but we must create an environment where students feel comfortable communicating their needs without embarrassment.

The Profound Benefits

Why is all this adaptation worthwhile? Because the benefits of continued karate training for senior practitioners are remarkable:

Physical benefits: Maintained flexibility, improved balance (reducing fall risk), sustained cardiovascular health, preservation of bone density through weight-bearing exercise, enhanced coordination, and maintained functional strength for daily activities.

Mental benefits: Improved cognitive function through learning complex patterns, enhanced focus and concentration, stress reduction, and a sense of continued growth and achievement.

Social benefits: Community connection, multigenerational interaction, shared purpose, and the dignity of being a valued dojo member.

Spiritual benefits: Continued pursuit of personal development, embodiment of the karate principle of "kaizen" (continuous improvement), and the deep satisfaction of lifelong learning.

Honouring the Journey

I've had the profound privilege of promoting students to black belt in their sixties and seventies. I've watched practitioners in their eighties execute kata with such precision and grace that it brings tears to my eyes. These students embody what karate truly means: dedication, perseverance, and the continuous refinement of self.

When we adapt training for senior practitioners, we're not diminishing karate—we're honoring its deepest principles. We're acknowledging that the essence of our art lies not in how hard you can hit or how high you can kick, but in the dedication you bring to continuous improvement, the respect you show to others, and the character you develop through disciplined practice.

Every student who walks into the dojo carrying arthritis, managing heart conditions, or negotiating the realities of aging, yet still choosing to train, deserves our deepest respect and our most thoughtful instruction. They remind us all that karate is truly a lifelong journey, one that continues to offer growth, challenge, and profound satisfaction regardless of age.

Our role as instructors is to ensure that journey continues safely, meaningfully, and with the dignity every dedicated practitioner deserves.

I am a Martial Artist
By Leanne Canning

I stand upon the mat so bare,
With empty hands and open air.
It's not for anger, strife, or fight,
But for a calm and steady light.

Some see a punch, a kick, a shout,
But what it means is deep, no doubt.
It's more than moves, a tricky game,
It gives my spirit a true name.

My body learns to stand up tall,
To answer every sudden call.
With muscles built and spirit bright,
I find a hidden, inner might.

Each stretch I do, each turn I make,
For strength and grace, my body wakes.
I learn to move with easy flow,
To let my hidden power grow.

My mind must learn to be quite still,
To focus with a strong, calm will.
No busy thoughts, no hurried race,
Just quiet strength in this quiet place.

It teaches me to be aware,
To breathe away all stress and care.
To listen close, to see things clear,
To face my doubts and conquer fear.

Image by Sucek

If danger comes, a shadow deep,
A promise that my training keeps.
To stand my ground, to be quite brave,
The skill to guard, the self to save.

Not to harm, but to be strong,
To know where I truly belong.
A confidence that grows inside,
Where fear and worry cannot hide.

I bow to those who teach and guide,
With humble heart and honest pride.
Respect for all, both old and new,
This simple rule, I hold it true.

To listen well, to learn and try,
To reach for goals that sit up high.
To know I'm small, but I can grow,
A seed of kindness, I will sow.

It is a path, a winding way,
I learn new lessons every day.
From white belt steps to black belt aim,
It's not a finish, just a name.

The journey is the joy for me,
To always strive, to always be
A better person than before,
And learn what life has waiting store.

In halls of wood, with friends so dear,
We share the sweat, we calm the fear.
A family built on common ground,
Where honest efforts can be found.

We help each other stand and rise,
With understanding in our eyes.
A bond that's strong, a helping hand,
Across the mat, throughout the land.

So why am I a martial artist, true?
It helps my spirit shine right through.
It brings me peace, a steady heart,
And makes me feel a brand new start.

A balance found, a quiet grace,
To find my strength in any place.
To master self, not just a move,
This is the reason I approve.

It's not about the medals won,
Or battles fought beneath the sun.
It's how I live, what I believe,
The good I give, the peace I weave.

So I will train, with mind and soul,
To make my spirit strong and whole.
This is my path, my chosen way,
A martial artist, every day.

by Leanne Canning

Women Aware Defence
NEVER GIVE UP THE FIGHT

Image by Sucek

My Outlook on Karatedo

Adaption, Evolution and the Freedom to Walk Your Own Path

by Brad Weston

The following is a collection of my personal observations of the state of Japanese karatedo. This is from my personal thoughts, experiences and interactions over the past 20 years here in Japan.

Introduction: Karatedo as a Living Way

Karatedo is more than just kata, kumite, or a collection of techniques. It is a path—a way of life. Yet too often, it becomes frozen in rigid forms, controlled by organisations, or claimed by instructors who confuse authority with ownership.

To me, karatedo must remain a living martial art. It must adapt to the student, evolve with the times, and never be something that can be owned.

My outlook on karatedo is simple: it should be a martial way of adaptation, evolution, and freedom.

Over the years, I have observed students struggle when forced into rigid styles. One student with a smaller frame could never replicate the traditional power stances exactly, yet their timing and precision were exceptional. By allowing them to adapt the techniques to their body, their skills flourished beyond what strict adherence would have allowed.

Adaptation: Karatedo for the Individual

Every student who steps into the dojo is unique. They bring with them different body types, mindsets, experiences, and even limitations. Yet too often, instructors force them into a single mold, as if karatedo were fixed and unchanging.

But karatedo should not demand that students adapt to it. Instead, karatedo must adapt to the student. The core principles—timing, distance, power, and intent—remain universal, but their expression will always look different from person to person.

This individuality is not weakness. It is karatedo's true strength.

When I first started teaching, I tried to make every student fit the same exact model. It caused frustration, injuries, and diminished confidence. Over time, I learned that stepping back and observing each student's natural tendencies, and then guiding them to refine what already worked for them, produced far greater results.

Tradition: Foundation or Prison?

Tradition connects us to the past, but not everything handed down deserves blind preservation. Sometimes flaws, inefficiencies, and gaps are defended under the name of "tradition."

We must remember: the masters we revere were innovators. They adapted, questioned, and reshaped karatedo to fit their world. If we fossilise karatedo in the name of tradition, we betray their spirit.

I visited a dojo once where the emphasis was solely on perfecting a series of forms exactly as they had been practiced for decades. Students were afraid to ask questions or explore alternatives. Many left frustrated, not because the art was flawed, but because their personal growth was stifled by rigid adherence.

Tradition should be a foundation to build upon, not a prison to trap us.

Teachers, Egos, and the Razor's Edge

The greatest obstacle in karatedo is not technique—it is ego.

As teachers, we must remember our true position. We are not gods, not bosses, not gurus. We are educators, walking a razor's edge. It is all too easy to slip into roles that grant power, feed egos, and deviate from "the way."

Over the decades, I have observed instructors who demanded absolute conformity. Students were discouraged from asking questions or experimenting with techniques. While their forms looked perfect on the outside, understanding was shallow, and confidence was stifled. I realized the ego of the teacher can unintentionally harm the very art we claim to uphold.

To be true to karatedo, we must push these temptations away. Our duty is to build our students, provide them with the best tools and resources, and celebrate when they take what we have given them and innovate further.

Teachers must also remain students. We must continue to train, refine, and learn. Each lesson, mistake, and moment of insight allows us to evolve. By doing so, our "way" remains alive—constantly changing, evolving, and, we hope, improving.

Karatedo as Personal Knowledge

When students practice, sweat, and refine, karatedo becomes theirs. It is not borrowed, not rented. The knowledge belongs to them.

Students should not simply copy their teacher. They should adapt karatedo to their own philosophy, ideals, and journey. This is how karatedo stays alive.

I remember a student who created a unique combination of footwork and strikes. At first, I questioned whether it deviated too far from tradition. But after observing them, it was clear they had internalised the principles perfectly—they were expressing them in a new way. Their innovation became their own signature, and it was a joy to witness.

A true teacher should feel pride, not fear, when a student branches off. No one owns karatedo. It belongs to those who walk it.

Conclusion: Stop Claiming Karatedo, Keep Walking the Way

Karatedo does not belong to a style, an organization, or a teacher. It belongs to those who practice it, adapt it, and live it.

Our duty as teachers is to educate, not to control. Our duty as students is to continue learning, refining, and growing.

By letting go of ownership, embracing change, and valuing individuality, karatedo can continue to be a living, breathing art that serves everyone who walks the path.

If we honor these truths, karatedo will remain what it has always been: a living way. Not frozen. Not claimed. But free.

And that, to me, is the spirit of Karatedo

A Marital Artists Essential Guide

Staying Hydrated Through the Australian Summer

by Maria Francis

Image by Signature Getty Images

Proper hydration isn't just important—it's the difference between a productive training session and a dangerous one. Whether you're practicing karate in Perth's scorching dry heat, training Brazilian jiu-jitsu in Brisbane's humidity, or perfecting your kata in Sydney's coastal summer, understanding hydration is fundamental to your performance, safety, and progression.

The Australian summer presents unique challenges for martial artists. We're not just dealing with warm weather; we're facing temperatures that regularly exceed 35°C, often combined with humidity levels that can make indoor dojo training feel like you're working out in a sauna. Add to this the intensity of martial arts training—the explosive movements, the sustained techniques, the mental focus required—and you've got a recipe for serious fluid loss that demands respect and strategy.

Understanding Why Hydration Matters
Your body is approximately 60% water, and this fluid is essential for virtually every function that keeps you alive and performing. During martial arts training, water regulates your body temperature through sweat, transports nutrients to working muscles, cushions your joints during those powerful kicks and throws, and enables the chemical reactions that produce energy. When you're even mildly dehydrated—losing just 2% of your body weight in fluids—your performance drops noticeably. Your reaction time slows, your power decreases, your endurance falters, and your mental focus wavers.

I've seen black belts with impeccable technique struggle through basic drills simply because they didn't prioritise hydration. The dojo floor can be unforgiving when you're running on empty, and in the Australian summer, "empty" can happen frighteningly fast.

The Science of Sweat and Fluid Loss
During a typical one-hour martial arts session in summer conditions, the average adult can lose between 0.5 to 2.5 litres of sweat—sometimes more during particularly intense training. Factors that increase sweat loss include higher temperatures, increased humidity, training intensity, your fitness level, body size, and individual sweat rate (which varies significantly between people).

What many martial artists don't realise is that sweat isn't just water. When you perspire, you're losing crucial electrolytes—primarily sodium, but also potassium, magnesium, and calcium. These minerals are essential for muscle contraction, nerve signalling, and maintaining proper fluid balance in your cells. This is why simply drinking water, while important, isn't always enough during extended or intense training sessions.

Your body has sophisticated mechanisms for maintaining hydration, but they work best when you support them proactively. Thirst is actually a late indicator of dehydration—by the time you feel thirsty during training, you're already behind the eight ball. As coaches, we need to train our students to hydrate strategically, not just reactively.

Pre-Training Hydration

Proper hydration starts well before you step onto the dojo floor. I recommend my students begin focusing on hydration at least 4-6 hours before training. This isn't about chugging massive amounts of water right before class (which can lead to discomfort and excessive bathroom breaks); it's about ensuring your body starts from a well-hydrated baseline.

A practical pre-training hydration strategy looks like this:

4-6 hours before training: drink 400-600ml of water. Your urine colour is an excellent indicator—aim for pale yellow, like light lemonade. Dark yellow or amber urine indicates you need more fluids.

2-3 hours before training: drink another 200-300ml. If it's going to be a particularly intense session or the forecast is for extreme heat, consider a drink containing electrolytes. 30 minutes before training: Have a final 200ml of water. This tops up your system without overloading your stomach.

On training days, pay attention to what you're eating as well. Foods with high water content—fruits like watermelon, oranges, and strawberries, or vegetables like cucumber and celery—contribute to your overall hydration status. Avoid excessive caffeine or alcohol in the hours before training, as both can have diuretic effects.

During Training: Strategic Hydration

This is where many martial artists either do too little or, occasionally, too much. The goal during training is to replace the fluids you're losing through sweat without overwhelming your system.

For sessions under one hour at moderate intensity, water is generally sufficient. I encourage students to drink 150-250ml every 15-20 minutes. Don't wait until the designated water break—if you need a quick sip during paired drills or technique practice, take it. A few seconds to hydrate is far better than compromised performance or heat stress. For sessions exceeding one hour, or particularly intense training in hot conditions, you need to think about electrolyte replacement. This is where sports drinks or electrolyte solutions become valuable. However—and this is crucial—you don't need to drink sports drinks for every training session. They contain sugar and calories that, while useful for energy during extended training, aren't necessary for a standard one-hour class.

I've developed a simple rule for my students: if you're training for less than an hour and you're well-nourished, stick with water. If you're training for longer than an hour, doing multiple sessions in a day, or training in extreme heat, incorporate electrolytes.

The key is consistency. Small, regular sips beat large, infrequent gulps every time. Your body can only absorb fluids at a certain rate, and flooding your stomach with liquid can lead to discomfort, cramping, and even nausea during intense movement.

Post-Training Recovery:

The work doesn't stop when class ends. Post-training hydration is essential for recovery and preparing your body for the next session.

A general guideline is to drink approximately 1.5 litres of fluid for every kilogram of body weight lost during training. You can track this by weighing yourself before and after training (in minimal clothing for accuracy).

For example, if you've lost 1kg during a two-hour training session, you should aim to consume 1.5 litres over the next few hours. This doesn't mean drinking it all at once—spread it out over the subsequent 2-4 hours for optimal absorption.

Post-training is an excellent time for electrolyte replacement, particularly if you've had an intense session or multiple training periods in one day. Many martial artists overlook this, but adequate sodium replacement after heavy sweating is crucial for proper rehydration. Your body can't retain water effectively without sufficient sodium.

Natural options include coconut water (which contains potassium and magnesium), milk (surprisingly effective for rehydration due to its electrolyte and protein content), or a piece of fruit with a small handful of salted nuts. Of course, purpose-designed sports drinks or electrolyte tablets work well too.

Understanding Electrolytes:
Let's break down what electrolytes actually do and why they matter for martial artists:
Sodium is the primary electrolyte lost in sweat and the most important for maintaining fluid balance. It helps your body retain water and maintains blood pressure and volume. During intense Australian summer training, sodium losses can be significant.

Potassium works in partnership with sodium to regulate fluid balance inside and outside cells. It's crucial for proper muscle contraction and preventing cramps. Bananas are famously rich in potassium, but so are potatoes, oranges, and spinach.

Magnesium is involved in over 300 enzymatic reactions in your body, including energy production and muscle function. Deficiency can lead to muscle cramps, weakness, and fatigue—all things martial artists can't afford.

Calcium isn't just for bone health; it's essential for muscle contraction and nerve signalling. While we don't lose as much calcium through sweat as other electrolytes, maintaining adequate levels is still important. The beauty of electrolyte balance is that you don't need expensive supplements if you're eating a varied, nutritious diet. However, during summer training, particularly in extreme conditions, supplementation can be beneficial. Look for products that provide a balanced mix of electrolytes without excessive sugar.

The Hidden Danger: Overhydration and Hyponatremia
Here's something that surprises many martial artists: you can actually drink too much water, and the consequences can be serious. Hyponatremia—dangerously low blood sodium levels—occurs when you drink excessive amounts of plain water without replacing lost electrolytes, effectively diluting your blood's sodium concentration.

Symptoms include nausea, headache, confusion, muscle weakness, seizures, and in severe cases, it can be life-threatening. I've witnessed martial artists, particularly beginners who've been told to "drink heaps of water," inadvertently putting themselves at risk by consuming excessive plain water during extended training without any electrolyte replacement.

The risk increases during very long training sessions, particularly in heat, when you're losing significant sodium through sweat but replacing it only with water. Endurance athletes are most at risk, but it can happen to anyone who drastically overdrinks.

How do you avoid it? Listen to your body, don't force excessive amounts of water beyond what feels comfortable, and ensure you're consuming electrolytes during extended training sessions. If you're urinating frequently and your urine is completely clear (like pure water), you may be overdoing it. Pale yellow is ideal—completely clear can indicate overhydration.

Practical Tips for Australian Martial Artists
Invest in a quality water bottle that you bring to every training session. Make it part of your kit, like your gi or gloves. I prefer insulated bottles that keep water cool throughout training.

Monitor your urine colour as your primary hydration indicator. It's simple, effective, and doesn't require any special equipment.

Weigh yourself before and after training occasionally to understand your typical sweat rate. This helps you personalise your hydration strategy.

Adjust for conditions. A 40°C day in Perth requires a different approach than a 25°C evening session in Melbourne. Pay attention to both temperature and humidity.

Don't rely on thirst alone. By the time you're thirsty during training, you're already somewhat dehydrated. Drink proactively, not reactively.

Consider timing. Training early morning or late evening during summer peaks can significantly reduce heat stress and fluid requirements.

Acclimatise gradually. If you've been training in air conditioning and suddenly switch to outdoor or non-air-conditioned training, give your body time to adapt over 7-14 days.
Watch for warning signs: Dizziness, excessive fatigue, muscle cramps, headache, decreased coordination, or dark urine all indicate hydration issues. Stop training and address them immediately.
Communicate with your instructor. Good coaches understand that hydration needs vary. Don't feel embarrassed about taking an extra water break if you need it.

Hydration as a Training Fundamental
In martial arts, we often talk about the fundamentals—proper stance, correct breathing, mental focus. Hydration deserves equal status. It's not supplementary to your

training; it's fundamental to it. Proper hydration enables everything else you're working to achieve: faster reactions, sustained power, mental clarity, injury prevention, and effective recovery.

The Australian summer will challenge you. The heat will test your resolve and your preparation. But with smart, strategic hydration practices, you can train safely and effectively regardless of what the thermometer reads. Your body is your primary tool in martial arts—treat it with the respect it deserves by keeping it properly fuelled with both water and electrolytes.

Remember, hydration isn't just about drinking water when you're thirsty. It's about understanding your body's needs, planning ahead, monitoring your status, and adjusting your approach based on conditions and training intensity. Master these skills as diligently as you master your techniques, and you'll find yourself training stronger, recovering faster, and progressing further in your martial arts journey.

Stay hydrated, train smart, and respect the Australian summer. Your body—and your martial arts practice—will thank you for it.

Image by Kieferpix

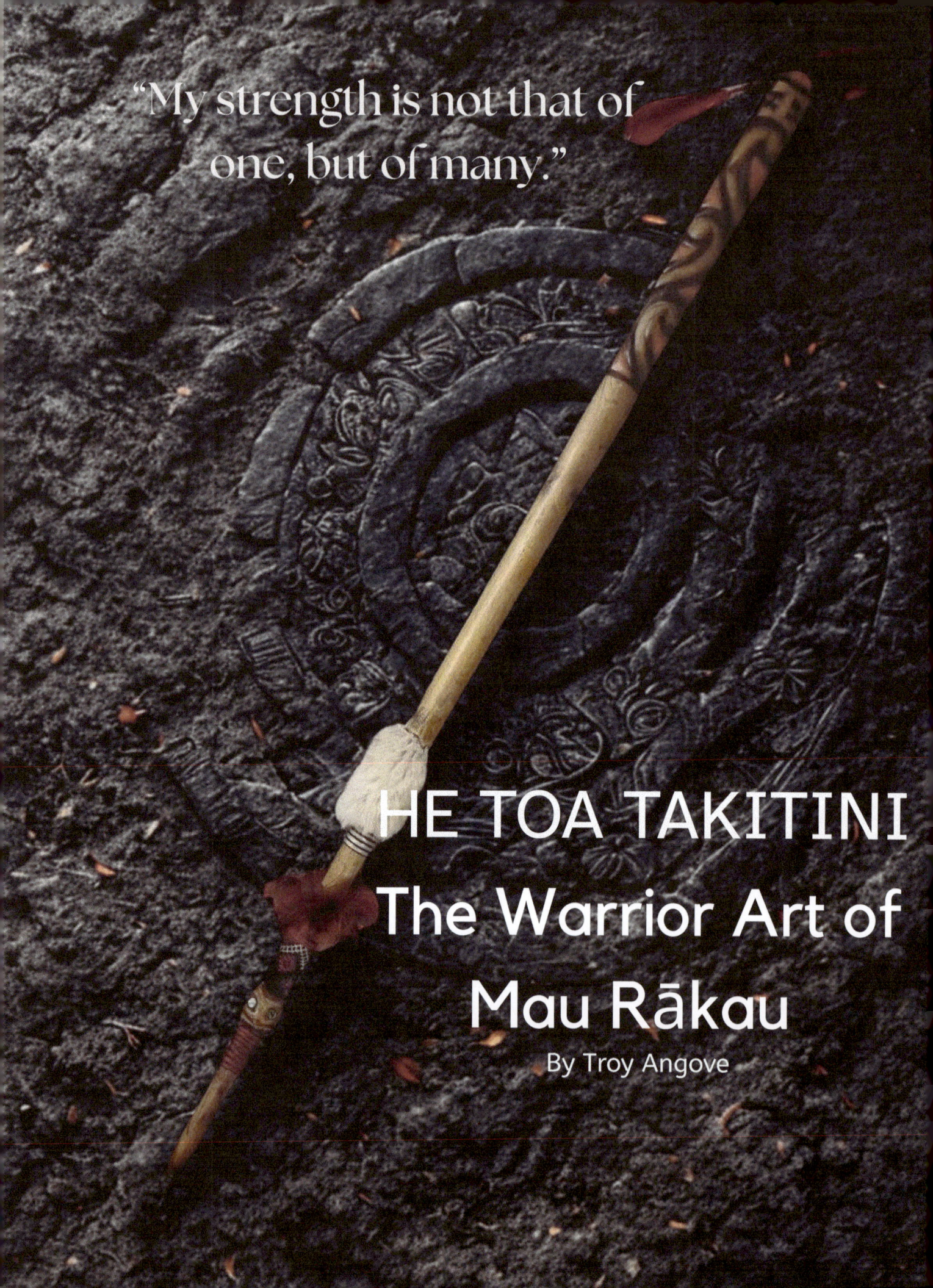

"My strength is not that of one, but of many."

HE TOA TAKITINI
The Warrior Art of Mau Rākau

By Troy Angove

I was raised within the Polynesian community of South Auckland—"Home of the Brave"—specifically in the notorious ward of Ōtara. My Martial Arts journey began at the age of seven, in 1985. Both of my parents were servicemen, my Mother in the Royal New Zealand Air Force (Te Tauaarangi o Aotearoa) and my Father in the New Zealand Army (Ngāti Tūmatauenga). My father also served alongside the Australian Army during the Vietnam campaign. Ko Troy Angove ahau (My name is Troy Angove).

I have spent most of my life in Martial Arts, learning under some of the best teachers in the world. However, I do not believe in building my reputation upon their names. The essence of Mau Rākau cannot be fully understood without knowledge of New Zealand culture and Te Reo Māori (Māori Language), but I will do my best to present it here in English.

Throughout my life I have studied several Martial Arts: Chinese Martial Arts in the greatest depth, but also Tae Kwon Do, Boxing, Filipino Stick Play, and a number of lesser-known disciplines. In 2000, I received a scholarship to study Martial Arts in Beijing, and ultimately spent ten years in China. In 2010, I was given formal permission to open my own schools, and I returned home to begin teaching.

My years in China were invaluable. I studied numerous hand-to-hand systems of Kung Fu, but what captivated me most was the study of weaponry. Chinese Martial Arts are renowned for their wide range of weapons, and during my time there I became proficient in dual swords, long pole, single stick, short knife, and nunchaku, among others.

My childhood was shaped by violence. South Auckland in the 1980s and 1990s was a rough place. I grew up in the shadows of older boys who used their hands to express anger—a reflection of the environment. I witnessed things no child should have to see. Weapons were a normal part of life: guns, knives, sticks of every kind, brass knuckles, SAP sticks, blackjacks. Violence, fighting, and beatings were expected. It was in this environment, around the age of ten, that I first encountered the art of Mau Rākau.

The art of Mau Rākau was forged through generations of conflict. Centuries of inter-tribal warfare shaped its techniques, strategies and combative principles. Before the arrival of Europeans, Māori warfare was conducted without the use of metal—wood, stone and bone were the primary materials used in crafting weapons.

Battles were fought at close range, making combat deeply personal and often brutal. From these conditions arose a complex system of customs, traditions and battlefield etiquette that guided how warriors trained, fought and conducted themselves.

Weapon training was an essential part of life for Māori men and began at a young age, ensuring that every generation carried forward the skills, discipline and knowledge necessary to protect their people and uphold their ancestral responsibilities.

Mau Rākau is a traditional Māori Martial Art. Its styles and customs vary across Tribes, though many modern schools share common principles. What follows is my personal and limited understanding of Mau Rākau from the northern regions of New Zealand (Aotearoa), particularly that of Ngāpuhi. The term Mau Rākau refers to "bearing arms" or "to wield weapons." Rākau can also mean tree, stick, or wood. While Mau Rākau includes many weapons, this writing focuses on one—the Taiaha.

The Taiaha is the weapon most commonly associated with the Māori warrior. It appears on New Zealand's coat of arms and is used in ceremonial greetings and important cultural events. Although often viewed as ceremonial, it is by no means limited to such use.

Taiaha vary widely in materials and length. Common woods include Rimu, Kauri, and Tōtara, though many other hardwoods were used depending on region. Bone was also used, particularly large whale bones carved into Taiaha. Paua (abalone) shell, prized for its shimmering green-blue colour, was often carved into small circles and set into the eyes of the weapon's carved head, giving it life. The Auckland War Memorial Museum (Tāmaki Paenga Hira) houses a number of notable Taiaha, ranging from 1.3 to over 2 metres in length.

A Taiaha is composed of several parts. At the bottom is the carved tongue (Arero), leading into the head (Upoko). Above this is the long shaft or body (Tinana), which begins rounded for the grip, then gradually widens and flattens toward the top. The upper end forms a blade (Rau), often 5–10cm wide. Māori carving served as a written language, and the carvings on the Arero and Upoko often represented ancestry or tribal origins. While some Taiaha were carved along their full length, most featured designs primarily at the head, sometimes with a decorated band near the top.

My upbringing—and the environment I grew up in—led me not only into Martial Arts but also toward my first exposure to Mau Rākau. Many of my childhood friends were part of a Kapa Haka group called Ngā Hau E Whā (The Four Winds), led by Kaumātua Ihimaera (Mr Ihimaera). They learned traditional dance, footwork, chants, haka, and weaponry. Through them, I first witnessed the movements and ideology behind many traditions.

Like many Eastern Martial Arts, Mau Rākau incorporates motions inspired by animals. Yet New Zealand's unique wildlife shaped these inspirations—there were no native land mammals except bats, so many movements reflect birds or reptiles. Other movements are based on gods, spirits, or ancestors.

My closest friend was fluent in Māori and assisted our school's Māori language teacher. As part of his education, he was sent to Mokoia Island in Rotorua to study Mau Rākau under Kaumātua Sharples (Mr Sharples). Mokoia Island, once a stronghold of Ngāti Whātua in the 1800s, was invaded in 1821 by a Ngāpuhi war party led by Hongi Hika. Hundreds were killed or enslaved, and deep-seated resentment lingered. Because of this history, Mokoia Island later became the spiritual training ground for modern Mau Rākau. When my friend returned from his training, he shared everything he had learned—my first true exposure to close- and mid-range techniques and the double-striking methods unique to the art.

Most styles of Mau Rākau are considered close-range systems. The postures (stances) are shaped by ancestral teachings (tikanga). The Taiaha itself is versatile, fast, graceful, and deadly. The blade end (Rau) delivers strikes with the weight of a large stick and the speed of a small one. Strikes can be sweeping, arcing, stabbing, or scraping, while defence relies on counter-striking with either end of the weapon. Footwork is critical for defence, and feints are essential for attack.

My formal study of Mau Rākau began in 2015, both at Te Wānanga o Aotearoa (The University of New Zealand) and on Marae (meeting grounds). A Marae is a place of belonging (Tūrangawaewae), where traditional skills such as song, weaving, carving, haka, and weaponry are taught. After nearly three decades studying Chinese Martial Arts, beginning Mau Rākau was enlightening. It helped me reconnect with my heritage and identity, and revealed a fighting system equal to any I had encountered.

Training in most Mau Rākau schools begins with foundational stances (Ahai), which act as ready positions or defensive forms. Students then learn combinations of blocks and counterattacks with basic stepping patterns. Once these fundamentals are solid, a significant amount of time is spent on footwork.

Much of this footwork mirrors the movements of birds—light, agile, requiring strong legs and consistent practice. Level changes, squatting, and jumping are common. Traditional stick games are practised in groups, and haka are recited between exercises.

In modern times, Mau Rākau has entered a sport-fighting environment. As with many weapon arts that adopt protective gear, some traditional techniques are sacrificed in favour of scoring points, sometimes at the cost of realistic defence. Nevertheless, it provides a safer path for the art to grow and evolve.

Mau Rākau is far more than a fighting system—it is a living expression of Māori culture, history, and identity. My journey into this art has been deeply personal, shaped by both the hardships of my upbringing and the discipline of decades spent studying Martial Arts around the world. While the Taiaha is often seen as ceremonial symbol, it remains a highly refined and effective weapon, rooted in ancestral knowledge and cultural significance.

To study Mau Rākau is to connect with the values, stories, movements, and spirit of New Zealand (Aotearoa). It has taught me not only how to move, but how to stand—how to understand where I come from, and how to honour those who came before me. Through Mau Rākau, I have rediscovered my heritage, strengthened my identity, and found a path that continues to challenge and inspire me every day.

My hope is that the Art of Mau Rākau and the customs associated with it will spread beyond the boarders of New Zealand (Aotearoa), transcending race and culture in the way that Eastern Martial Arts have, Mau Rākau bridges ancient New Zealand tradition and Martial skills into a modern age, a skill which was nearly lost due to European suppression and the introduction of the firearm.

As of 2025 I moved to Brisbane Australia. My school "Wing Chun Kung Fu New Zealand" is still operating in South Auckland New Zealand by my students Asmeet Prakash and Henare Waru. We can be contacted via email on wingchunkungfu@hotmail.com.

Thank you for allowing me the opportunity to share my limited knowledge and understanding on this subject.
Ngā mihi nui.

Teaching with Understanding
Supporting Students with Learning Difficulties in Martial Arts

by Thierry Rose

Image by Shironosov Getty Images

Any martial arts instructor is privileged to teach students from all walks of life, each bringing their unique strengths, challenges, and learning styles to the dojo. Among our most rewarding teaching experiences are often those involving students with learning difficulties—children and adults who may process information differently, struggle with certain aspects of traditional instruction, or require adapted teaching approaches to reach their full potential.

Over my years of running traditional karate dojos, I've taught students with dyslexia, ADHD, autism spectrum conditions, dyspraxia, auditory and visual processing disorders, and various other learning differences. What I've discovered is this: martial arts training offers extraordinary benefits for these students, and with thoughtful adaptation of our teaching methods, these practitioners often excel in ways that surprise everyone—sometimes most of all themselves.

This article explores practical strategies instructors can employ to support students with learning difficulties, home practice techniques that reinforce dojo learning, and most importantly, how to create an inclusive environment where every student can thrive.

Understanding Learning Differences
First, let's establish some foundational understanding. "Learning difficulties" or "learning differences" encompasses a broad spectrum of neurological variations that affect how individuals process, retain, and express information. These are not indicators of intelligence—many individuals with learning difficulties have average or above-average intelligence. They simply process information differently.

Common learning differences we encounter in martial arts settings include: Dyslexia: Primarily affects reading and language processing, but can also impact sequencing, directions (left/right), and memory for verbal instructions.

ADHD (Attention Deficit Hyperactivity Disorder): affects attention, impulse control, and executive function. Students may struggle with sustained focus, following multi-step instructions, or waiting their turn.

Autism Spectrum Conditions: present in diverse ways, but commonly involve differences in social communication, sensory processing, preference for routine and predictability, and sometimes motor coordination challenges.

Dyspraxia (Developmental Coordination Disorder): Affects motor planning and coordination. Students may struggle with learning physical sequences, bilateral coordination, or spatial awareness.

Auditory Processing Disorder: difficulty processing spoken language, particularly in noisy environments or when instructions are lengthy.

Visual Processing Disorder: difficulty interpreting visual information, which can affect learning from demonstrations or reading body language.

Working Memory Difficulties: challenges holding multiple pieces of information in mind while working with them, affecting the ability to follow multi-step instructions.

It's crucial to remember that these conditions often co-occur, and every individual presents differently. A teaching approach that works brilliantly for one student with ADHD might need significant modification for another with the same diagnosis. The key is individualisation within a group setting.

Before we discuss adaptations, let's acknowledge why martial arts is particularly beneficial for students with learning differences:

Structure and routine: the predictable structure of martial arts classes—the same opening ceremony, similar warm-up patterns, consistent expectations—provides security for students who thrive on routine.

Physical expression: for students who struggle with verbal or written expression, martial arts offers a physical language through which they can excel and communicate.

Immediate feedback: the physical nature of martial arts provides instant, concrete feedback. You either maintain balance or you don't; the technique either works or it doesn't. This clarity helps students who struggle with abstract concepts.

Multisensory learning: martial arts naturally incorporates visual (demonstration), auditory (instruction), and kinaesthetic (physical practice) learning, benefiting students regardless of their primary learning style.

Self-regulation: the controlled, disciplined nature of training helps develop executive function skills and emotional regulation.
Success experiences: many students with learning difficulties have experienced repeated academic frustration. Martial arts offers a fresh arena where they can experience success and competence.

Confidence building: as students master techniques and progress through ranks, they develop genuine self-confidence that transfers to other life areas.

Visual Strategies
Demonstration over explanation: show rather than tell whenever possible.

Demonstrate techniques multiple times from different angles. Many students with learning differences are strong visual learners.

Visual schedules and routines: display the class structure visually—pictures or simple text showing warm-up, kata practice, partner work, cool-down. This helps students anticipate transitions and reduces anxiety.

Video resources: record yourself performing kata or techniques that students can watch at home. Slow-motion video is particularly helpful for breaking down complex movements.

Mirror technique: stand facing the same direction as students (rather than facing them) when demonstrating, so they can mirror your movements exactly without mentally reversing left and right.

Visual cues on the floor: use tape or markers to indicate spacing, positioning, or direction for students who struggle with spatial awareness.

Colour coding: use coloured tape or markers to distinguish left from right, or to indicate different sections of kata. For example, "Execute the red section of the kata."

Auditory Strategies

Clear, concise language: Avoid lengthy explanations. Use short, direct instructions: "Step forward. Punch. ."

Reduce background noise: minimise distractions during instruction. Turn off music, close doors, and ensure students are far from external noise sources when learning new material.

Consistent terminology: use the same words for techniques every time. If you call it "reverse punch" one day and "gyaku-zuki" the next, students with auditory processing difficulties may not connect them as the same technique.

Verbal chunking: break complex sequences into small chunks. Teach three moves, practice them repeatedly, then add the next three.

Rhythm and counting: many students benefit from rhythmic counting or verbal cues that match movements: "Step-punch-chamber-down."

Check for understanding: after giving instructions, ask a student to repeat them back in their own words. This isn't testing—it's ensuring the message was received.

Kinaesthetic Strategies

Hands-on guidance: with permission, physically guide students through movements. Proprioceptive input (the feeling of their body position) helps many students understand techniques better than visual or verbal instruction alone.

Repetition, repetition, repetition: students with learning differences often need significantly more repetitions to consolidate motor patterns. This isn't failure—it's how their nervous systems learn.

Breaking it down: isolate individual components of techniques. Practice just the hip rotation, then just the arm movement, then combine them.

Bilateral integration activities: for students with dyspraxia or coordination difficulties, include exercises that develop bilateral coordination: alternating punches, cross-body movements, mirror movements.

Balance and body awareness: incorporate specific balance exercises and activities that develop proprioception and body awareness.

Organisational and Executive Function Support
Predictable structure: maintain consistent class routines. Unexpected changes can be very challenging for some students.

Advance warning of transitions: "In five minutes, we'll finish kata and start partner work." This helps students who struggle with transitions.

Visual timers: use a visible timer for activities with time limits. This helps students gauge time and prepare for transitions.

Social and Emotional Support
Clear behavioral expectations: Explicitly teach dojo etiquette and social expectations. Don't assume students intuitively understand unwritten social rules.

Social stories: for students with autism spectrum conditions, create simple "social stories" explaining what to expect in specific situations (testing, tournaments, belt ceremonies).

Designated safe space: allow students who become overwhelmed to take brief breaks in a designated calm area.
Pair thoughtfully: when assigning partners, consider compatibility. Pair students with learning difficulties with patient, supportive partners.

Celebrate effort, not just outcomes: recognise hard work and improvement, regardless of absolute performance level.
Private feedback: some students struggle with public correction. Provide sensitive feedback privately when possible.

Specific Adaptations for Common Challenges

For Students with ADHD
Movement breaks: build in brief, vigorous movement breaks between segments requiring sustained focus.

Positioning: place students where you can easily redirect their attention—usually front and centre, or where you can make easy eye contact.

Clear start and stop signals: use a specific sound or gesture for "begin" and "stop" that's consistent and distinctive.

Channel energy: give leadership roles or responsibilities that channel energy positively: demonstrating techniques, counting for others, holding equipment.

Novelty and variety: while maintaining overall structure, incorporate variety within segments to maintain interest.

Immediate positive reinforcement: catch students doing well and acknowledge it immediately and specifically.

For Students on the Autism Spectrum
Sensory considerations: be aware of sensory sensitivities. Bright lights, loud kiai, physical contact, or certain textures might be overwhelming. Work with parents to understand individual sensitivities.

Advance preparation: inform students ahead of time about changes to routine, special events, or new activities.

For Students with Dyspraxia
Motor planning support: break every technique into the smallest possible components and practice each component in isolation before combining.

Extra time: allow additional time for learning new motor patterns. Don't rush progression.

Visual-verbal-physical combination: demonstrate while describing while physically guiding—triple reinforcement. Slow motion practice: encourage very slow execution initially to develop motor patterns correctly.

Over-learning: once a skill is acquired, practice it extensively to consolidate the motor pattern.

Crossing midline: include specific exercises that practice crossing the body's midline, which can be challenging for students with dyspraxia.

Home Practice Strategies
One of the most valuable supports instructors can provide is helping students practice effectively at home. Home practice reinforces dojo learning and accelerates progress.

Creating Home Practice Resources
Personal practice videos: record each

student performing their current kata or techniques. They can watch themselves at home, noting what to improve.

Instructor demonstration videos: provide video of yourself performing techniques students are working on. Keep these short and focused—one kata per video, not everything at once.

Written/pictorial sequences: create simple visual guides showing kata sequences with stick figures or photos, using minimal text.

Audio cues: for students who respond well to auditory input, create recordings of you counting through kata or calling techniques.

Practice checklists: provide simple lists of what to practice: "5 minutes stance work, 3 repetitions of kata, 10 kicks each leg."

Home Practice Recommendations for Parents
Establish routine: practice at the same time and place daily, even if briefly. Routine supports success.

Keep it short: for younger children or those with attention difficulties, 10-15 minutes of focused practice is better than 45 minutes of distracted effort.

Specific focus: rather than "practice everything," assign specific focus areas: "This week, practice just the first section of your kata."

Use mirror: practicing in front of a mirror provides visual feedback and helps students self-correct.

Create space: ensure adequate, safe space for practice. Remove breakables and ensure appropriate flooring.

Record practice: parents can video practice sessions so students can watch themselves, and instructors can review progress.

Incorporate fun: make some practice playful—target practice with pool noodles, balance games, technique races against a timer.

Parent involvement: when appropriate, parents can learn alongside children. This supports practice and builds family connection.

Celebrate improvement: help students recognise their own progress by comparing videos over time or keeping achievement journals.

Specific Home Exercises
Balance training: practice standing on one foot while performing upper body techniques. Start with eyes open, progress

to eyes closed. Use different surfaces (carpet, tile, foam pad).

Stance strengthening: hold stances for increasing durations. Start with 10 seconds, progress to 30, then 60. Focus on correct form, not just endurance.

Slow kata: practice kata in extreme slow motion, maintaining perfect balance throughout. This develops control and body awareness.

Mirror matching: practice techniques facing a mirror and try to make both sides look identical.

Count-along kata: practice kata while counting out loud, coordinating movement with counting. This develops rhythm and sequencing.

Visualisation practice: for students with physical limitations, mental practice (visualising performing techniques perfectly) has been shown to improve actual performance.

Flexibility routine: gentle, consistent stretching addressing specific flexibility needs.

Successful support of students with learning difficulties requires partnership with parents and caregivers.

Initial conversation: When enrolling a student with learning differences, have a private conversation with parents to understand:
- The specific nature of their child's learning difference
- What strategies work well in other settings
- What challenges they anticipate
- Any sensory sensitivities or triggers
- Any relevant medical considerations
- How the child communicates when overwhelmed or struggling

Ongoing communication: maintain regular contact about progress, challenges, and adjustments. A brief message after class: "Great focus today on kata!" or "Struggled a bit with partner work—any ideas about what might help?" shows you're attentive and collaborative.

Celebrate progress: share successes with parents, not just challenges. Students with learning differences have often heard extensively about their difficulties. Highlighting achievements builds family morale.

Coordinate strategies: if something works well at home or school, incorporate it in the dojo. If a dojo strategy is successful, share it with parents for home use.

Professional boundaries: instructors aren't therapists or educational specialists. If concerns arise beyond your expertise, recommend appropriate professional assessment.

Creating an Inclusive Dojo Culture
Beyond individual adaptations, the overall dojo culture profoundly impacts students with learning differences.

Celebrate diversity: explicitly communicate that everyone learns differently and that's not just okay—it's valuable. Different perspectives and approaches enrich the dojo community.
Educate all students: age-appropriately teach all students about learning differences, building empathy and understanding.

Zero tolerance for mockery: make it absolutely clear that mocking, teasing, or excluding anyone for any reason is unacceptable.

Highlight varied strengths: point out different students' strengths—technical precision, creativity, perseverance, kindness, power, flexibility. Show that there are many ways to excel.

Adjust expectations thoughtfully: maintain high standards while recognising that progression timelines may differ. A student might need twice as long to earn their next belt, and that's fine.

Inclusive language: use phrases like "learning differences" rather than "disabilities." Focus on what students can do, not what they can't.

The Instructor's Mindset
Perhaps most important is the mindset we bring to teaching students with learning differences.

Patience: learning may be slower, more non-linear, and require more repetition. That's the process, not a problem.

Creativity: be willing to try different approaches. If visual demonstration doesn't work, try tactile guidance. If that doesn't work, try verbal cues, or analogies, or... Keep experimenting.

Belief: genuinely believe these students can succeed. Your expectations powerfully influence their performance.

Growth mindset: model and teach that abilities develop through effort. "You haven't mastered this yet" emphasises the learning process.

Individualisation: remember that disability labels describe categories, not individuals. Get to know each student's unique learning profile.

Humility: be willing to learn from students, parents, and specialists about what works. You don't need to have all the answers.

The Profound Impact
I've watched students with significant learning differences achieve remarkable

things in martial arts. I've seen the child who couldn't sit still in school spend 45 minutes in focused kata practice. I've seen the teenager who struggled with every academic subject earn his black belt through sheer determination. I've seen the young person who felt incompetent in every other domain discover genuine competence and confidence in the dojo.

These successes didn't happen because I was an exceptional teacher or because martial arts is magic. They happened because we created an environment where different ways of learning were accepted and supported, where effort was celebrated, where struggle was normalised, and where every student genuinely belonged.

Teaching students with learning differences isn't about lowering standards or feeling sorry for them. It's about recognising that intelligence and capability come in many forms, that there are multiple paths to excellence, and that our role as instructors is to help each student find their path.

When we do this work thoughtfully and compassionately, we don't just teach martial arts techniques. We build confidence, develop capabilities, create community, and sometimes, we change lives. That's the profound privilege and responsibility of being a martial arts instructor—for all our students, but perhaps especially for those who've struggled to find their place in more conventional settings.

> Every student deserves excellent instruction. Every student deserves to experience success. Every student deserves to belong. With understanding, adaptation, and genuine commitment to inclusive teaching, we can make that a reality in our dojos.

My Martial Arts Mentor
by Leanne Canning

Let me tell you about my martial arts mentor and how he impacted my life. Stepping into Alan's dojo for the first time, I felt something intangible yet powerful. The space buzzed with quiet focus and unmistakable energy. This intensity wasn't intimidating, it was inviting. From the first moment Alan greeted me, I knew this wasn't just about learning martial arts. It was about challenging myself on every level.

Alan wasn't just skilled; he was magnetic. His calm but razor-focused demeanour set the tone. He wasn't loud or demanding. Instead, his presence commanded attention effortlessly. His words were precise, never wasted. Whether he was instructing or simply observing, everything he did seemed to radiate purpose.

What stood out the most? It wasn't his unbeatable technique but the way he spoke to everyone—calm, direct, always encouraging. He had the ability to look you in the eye and make you believe you could achieve more than you thought possible. For Alan, martial arts was never just about punches, kicks or forms; it was about building better humans. Or as he would say, "We are not here to be mediocre, but invincible in our own mindset. "His enthusiasm for seeing his practitioners succeed pushed everyone, not just physically but mentally.

What stood out the most? It wasn't his unbeatable technique but the way he spoke to everyone—calm, direct, always encouraging. He had the ability to look you in the eye and make you believe you could achieve more than you thought possible. For Alan, martial arts was never just about punches, kicks or forms; it was about building better humans. Or as he would say, "We are not here to be mediocre, but invincible in our own mindset. "His enthusiasm for seeing his practitioners succeed pushed everyone, not just physically but mentally.

You could call him "stern," but it was more nuanced than that. He drew a fine line between toughness and compassion. If you missed a technique, Alan wouldn't let you off the hook. But he also wouldn't let you doubt yourself. Every correction wasn't criticism; it was an investment in your growth. That confidence in his teaching, even on day one, hooked me immediately.

Alan's approach to martial arts was a masterclass in mental discipline. He used every opportunity to strengthen not just the muscles in my body but the resilience and focus on my mind. His coaching went beyond kicks and stances, it was about conquering the thought patterns that often held me back. Time and time again, Alan stressed that martial arts begins in the mind. "Your mind controls everything else," he'd say. And he was right.

One of the greatest lessons I learned under Alan was how to face my mental barriers. He'd remind me everything begins with overcoming internal resistance. Those moments when fear and doubt tell you to stop before you even try. Once, during a tough advanced grappling drill, I hesitated. Alan immediately picked up on it. "What's stopping you right now doesn't exist outside of your mind," he said. I still hear those words.

There were many challenges like this in the dojo. Sparring against more advanced students, learning techniques I thought were "too complicated," and even training when I was physically exhausted. Alan would guide me through, never lowering the bar, but always helping me realise I could rise to meet it. Small victories turned into massive shifts in how I approached difficulties in life.

Training under Alan wasn't just about technique—it was about endurance, power and tenacity. Every session was reinforcement of how physical performance connects to mental resolve. Kicks, punches and exercises weren't standalone actions; they were tools to master personal growth.

Alan established a structured training regimen that emphasised consistency. Classes were three times a week: hour long yet intense. Each session began with warm-ups designed to increase flexibility and reduce injury risks. Squats, push-ups and dynamic stretches or as Alan called them, the fundamentals.

We cycled through drills focusing on precision and power. Striking pads sharpened our strikes, while sparring trained reaction times as well as resilience. By week's end, soreness was guaranteed, but so was a sense of improvement. Alan liked to say, "You'll feel this. But in time, it'll feel like progress, not pain."

Discipline wasn't handed out, it was earned through countless repetitions. Each punch, each block, each movement became second nature. For Alan, repetition wasn't boring; it was where mastery lived. "Any fool can hit hard once," he'd remind us, "but true skill is control you build one repetition at a time."

Alan crafted a teaching method where techniques were broken down step-by-step. While perfecting a roundhouse kick, he'd have us execute it over and over. First with focus on foot placement, then body coordination and later speed.

Sparring was one of Alan's favourite tools to teach us about fear. My first time sparring was unforgettable and honestly, overwhelming. I was matched with a more experienced student who didn't go easy on me. Each punch and kick came faster than I could react. My heart raced. My instincts screamed at me to step back, to play it safe.

But Alan was there, watching. He noticed the hesitation and said something simple but powerful: "Fear isn't your enemy, it's your teacher. Keep going." His words broke through the mental fog. I made it through the round—not gracefully, but I finished. Later, he explained how sparring teaches you to embrace discomfort, to expect chaos and still move forward.

Alan's mentorship extended far beyond the boundaries of the dojo. It shaped fundamental values, challenging me to become a better person in every aspect of life. Two central teachings stood out profoundly: the power of perseverance and the grace of respect.

One of Alan's most valuable lessons was that nothing worthwhile comes without effort. Martial arts practice continually pushes me to dig deeper, both physically and mentally. He would say, "The moments you want to quit are the moments you grow." Every sparring match and training drill emphasised this truth.

Alan's emphasise on showing up, regardless of excuses. Some days, I felt exhausted before even stepping into the dojo. Yet Alan's quiet expectation of presence was enough to keep me going. The lesson was clear: discipline isn't easy, but it's always rewarding. And just like in martial arts, perseverance in life creates lasting strength.

One of Alan's mottos was, "Never underestimate anyone, especially yourself." It often reminded me to treat others with dignity—whether they were more skilled, just starting or somewhere in between. Martial arts removed the ego, forcing everyone to grasp that no one grows in isolation. Respect acted as the foundation of trust: the partner holding pads for your punches today might help you perfect a complex grappling move tomorrow.

Looking back, Alan's influence stretches far beyond the dojo's mats. It wasn't just punches and kicks that reshaped my life. It was his philosophy on discipline, respect and the power of perseverance. Alan doesn't just train his practitioners ; he challenges us to think differently about who we are and what we could become. Every bit of advice given, every critique offered, wasn't limited to martial arts—it worked its way into my everyday life.

The life skills Alan imparted transcend martial arts. He taught perseverance, respect and mental clarity. Core principles for success anywhere. His lessons go far deeper than the surface:

Accountability: Alan believed in consistent accountability. Whether that meant perfecting a technique or correcting a mistake, excuses were irrelevant. This standard influenced how I took responsibility for my life, from career growth to personal relationships.

Humility and Confidence: confidence without arrogance is what Alan practices and preaches. This balance made me better in how I approached success and failure.

Every lesson Alan taught at the dojo doubled as a metaphor for life challenges. Wax-on-wax-off moments weren't just movie tropes, they mirrored real events. For example:

Steady Growth Over Quick Gains: Alan emphasised progress over perfection. The same principle transformed how I tackle long-term goals. It's all about small steps every day.

Facing Resistance: whether in sparring or life, resistance teaches us to adapt and grow calm under pressure. Martial arts is about solving, not avoiding, complex movements, just like problem-solving difficult situations in everyday routines.

Through Alan's mentorship, a subtle but profound shift happened, my perspective on what defines "personal success." I stopped measuring it by external markers like praise or rankings. Instead, I began looking inward, asking, "Am I better today than yesterday?" Alan taught that progress is deeply personal and doesn't require anyone's approval but our own.

> "Any fool can hit hard once, but true skill is control you build one repetition at a time."

The Sham-an
by Sam Dennett

Let's delve into my time with my first Jiu-Jitsu instructor.

I met MJ in 2020 at the darkest point in my life. I was chock full of depression, fear, and sadness. I had only just decided not to kill myself. He ran what started as a men's mental health organisation - a place for men like me to find support and attempt to heal trauma that blokes often experience - yet rarely talk about.

The type of trauma that gets bottled up and pushed down deep inside for fear of being ridiculed or judged. The type of trauma that, in my case, led me to believe that jumping off a cliff was the best course of action. The type of trauma that only a person with the correct, medical qualifications should approach. The type of credentials that MJ, did in fact, not have.

Over the next couple of years, this harmless support group morphed into a full-blown cult, causing an equal amount of damage as he claimed to heal. Delusions of grandeur, a Messiah-complex, blinded loyal followers, Moon worship, good men being completely broken down and rebuilt in His image, and a staggering amount of organisation rebrands that would make Elon Musk erect.

It was only a matter of time before he turned his attention to Martial Arts - an industry already rife with predators, abuse of power and cult-like behaviour.

I had left the main cult and distanced myself from MJ. However, I was (and still) in contact with a lot of the normal guys I had befriended through the group. One of these lads, who we'll refer to as 'D' had been preaching the good word about this Jiu-Jitsu stuff for a while, and decided to get a small group of blokes together to teach us the gentle art. Initially, I was reluctant - deathly afraid of any kind of violence since being assaulted and almost killed. Plus I'd been knocked out a fair few times during my life and wasn't too hyped on the idea of starting another combat sport in my thirties.

Eventually, I relented and told D I'd give him two months. And thus, my love of the sport was born.

Training with D and the boys was amazing. He ran a brilliant class, and I soon went from quite literally running away from my partner to getting stuck right in - keen as mustard to figure this grappling stuff out. It lit a fire in me I didn't know I was missing.

But, like everything MJ touches, it soon went to shit.

D and MJ were close - D was pretty much his right-hand man for a long time. Until he wasn't. Something happened within the inner circle and MJ got rid of him, amongst others. He had, however, been learning Jiu-Jitsu from D for a year or so and decided that he was more qualified than a legitimate brown belt, and took over the group as the new coach. Before this all went down, I had already gone and signed up for a further twelve months - under the assumption it would be D leading the charge.

I was a bit stuck; I loved our group and loved this sport. I was still a bit weary of MJ. But, he seemed to have relaxed a little bit, changing for the better that only something like Martial Arts can do. I mean, Tae Kwon Do taught me discipline, respect and integrity as a young boy, perhaps it would be the same for him?

Nope.

MJ fitted his garage with mats, a ramshackle set-up that I mentioned in a previous post, which I still think was a pretty cool start to my training. The added risk of cracking your head open on the concrete provided a Fight Club-esque atmosphere that did end up being quite a unique introduction to Jiu-Jitsu, but probably didn't go toward justifying the $400 per month price he was charging us.

MJ had taken the liberty of giving himself a purple belt after his year of training - as he'd pretty much been doing it full-time, he felt his skills were at an adequate level to award himself something that would take a normal person five, maybe six years. But MJ is no normal man - remember the above-mentioned delusions of grandeur? Yeah... I should have seen it coming, red flag number one. I imagine he somehow convinced D to 'award' him said belt, manipulating him as he'd done so effectively with many people before.

Red flag number two was that he didn't actually teach us anything. We would turn up at his house and just, roll. That's it. No shrimping, no framing, no pin escapes, not even a bloody concept we could try and apply. It was the ultimate ecological approach - although I think even Greg Souders would at least put some constraints on our games. This meant we would just do the same things over and over each week - making the same mistakes, which he took great pleasure in exploiting when it came to his turn to roll with us.

I remember one round against him where he shot under my hips and reaped me with all his might - for those who don't know; a reap is a technique that twists the receiver's knee inwards, exposing the foot for a devastating submission called a heel hook. Reaping is banned in a lot of beginner-level competitions. Even to this day, no one has ever reaped me that hard, yet here he was -

violently attacking my leg - an unsuspecting beginner, and I was paying him for the privilege. I didn't even know what a fucking leg lock was and all of a sudden I'm fighting for my ACL.

He couldn't even teach us how to defend stuff like this - because he didn't know anything. If any of us had a question about a technique, it would be deflected - we were told not to worry about it, or it would be some half-assed bullshido shite. For example, the only effective defence for a d'arce choke, according to him, was to firmly knock the elbow of the strangler, which we ate up like grateful dogs, thankful he would be so gracious to show us the defence to this choke he had been hitting on us for weeks. Now any Jiu-Jitsu player would tell you there's a lot more involved in defending that particular move - with popping the elbow being a very, very last-ditch attempt to not be rendered unconscious.

Red flag number three is a classic! We had to clean the mats ourselves after each session, and get this, take his bins out. Christ, that one is embarrassing.

Random bits of brand-new gym equipment would appear in the garage and his house. Balance boards, ankle weights, slant boards, medicine balls, plates etc. He would also brag about rolling with Jeremy Skinner every week - one of the best grapplers in Australia. It wasn't long before it clicked where our money was going; it was funding his private lessons and decking out his own gym. A gym he would always make a point of saying we could use any time.

"If you guys are a bit sore or whatever, feel free to come and just use the equipment and get a workout in, or feel free to come early and use anything you like."

One evening I did turn up early - only to be scolded as he needed time before each lesson to sit in silence/plan the lesson/workout solo, apparently. So I just, like, sat quietly for a bit until 6:30pm when the other boys arrived and it wasn't so uncomfortable.

Then it started to get weird.

The habits and behaviour that had turned me away from the main cult were starting to creep into this. MJ would start to pontificate about how he was starting to become SO good that he was inventing moves, how what we were doing wasn't Jiu-Jitsu - it was in fact a brand new Martial Art.

That's right, we were no longer practising Jiu-Jitsu, we were a part of something so cutting edge, so new, the world wasn't ready for what he had in store. He was going to change Martial Arts forever; he was going to "put Jiu-Jitsu out of business". He dubbed this new way of grappling 'Zoo Zoo'.

He began to rename all of the positions - I once called Ashi Garami by the English name; single leg X and he got annoyed and told me not to call it that. Instead, the seated guard became '1'. Shin-on-shin became '2'. Single leg - sorry, Ashi Garami, became '3'. I can't even begin to say how complicated this made things; Jiu-Jitsu names are confusing (just look at all the different names for the saddle, for example) however there is a slight semblance of sense to most (shin-on-shin being pretty self-explanatory).

The gatekeeping stepped up - other local players were gossiped about. I won't name anyone in particular, but I have since met and trained with some of these guys and they're lovely people who were more than willing to help out a middle-aged blue belt like me. I wasn't allowed to watch certain YouTube channels - he specifically called me out once when chatting about the latest B-Team video.

"You have to stop watching that shit, Sam"

At one point he told us that most of our learning was going to be through his pre-approved collection of instructional content on BJJ Fanatics, it was a complete cop out. Expecting people with full time jobs, children and relationships to watch a 7 hour DVD of Gordon Ryan's pin escapes - effectively teaching themselves, was ludicrous.

I wasn't even allowed to keep my blue belt! After our first competition, a few of us were awarded our blue belts. I was promoted, but because I vaped, he wouldn't let me keep the physical belt until I quit. I was allowed to display it in the garage as an incentive to pack in the vapes; a constant reminder that this man aims to control every aspect of my life.

Of course, I didn't leave the belt there. I earned that thing, so I took it anyway.

He decided the current belt system was stupid - the plan was to completely remove brown, and introduce grey. It would go: Grey, White, Blue, Purple, Black.

Black would be extremely rare - only for world-class athletes who would inevitably be drawn to our complete grappling art. A black belt would even be taken away from someone if they were no longer considered elite practitioners. Purple, he told us, would be the highest any of us could achieve as we were far too old to ever reach the pinnacle of the sport.

Then, the cherry on top, the pièce de résistance:

HE GAVE HIMSELF A BLACK BELT.

Yes, my friends, you did read that correctly. During our blue belt ceremony, not to be outshone by hobbyists, announced proudly that he had achieved black belt status.

"Uh...That's sick man, congrats" I managed to say, cutting through the awkward silence that blanketed the room.

This guy dared to give himself one of the highest honours in the sport. A feat that takes the average person around a decade of blood, sweat and tears to achieve. The audacity was absolutely mind-blowing. After just two years of training, a weekly private lesson with Jeremy, zero competition experience and beating up white belts, he had indeed reached the pinnacle of absurd.

Now, in the modern game, we've seen some very talented, hard-working people reach this milestone quicker than most; [Kit Dale], [Nicky Rod] and [Josh Saunders] to name a few. It is of course possible, but MJ isn't under the tutelage of world-class coaches or in a room full of killers. He's a 30-something bloke living in middle-class suburbia running a cult.

I was in the presence of an actual child. Remember that kid who just couldn't accept losing a make-believe game at school? The kid who would change the rules of the game to suit himself?

"No! You can't fly because my superpower stops you from flying and I can fly instead and I have guns that go through your armour and stops any attacks that you do"

"Ok, well I'll go into my bunker and hide from your powers"

"NO! THAT'S MY BUNKER YOU CAN'T HIDE THERE BECAUSE IT'S MINE NOW PLUS IT DOESN'T BLOCK MY POWERS IT BLOCKS YOURS BECAUSE I PUT A SPECIAL FORCE FIELD AROUND IT"

I was stunned. I made up my mind there and then I was going to move on, and started researching gyms that same evening.

We still had a few sessions left, though. Leaving the main cult was awkward enough; now I had to navigate getting out of this second one! And to be super honest, I was slightly scared. MJ is a very charming and clever guy - he could sell snow to Inuits.

That's the hallmark of great cult leaders - charisma, charm, and intelligence being some of their main weapons in influencing people. I didn't want to give him, or his die-hard disciples a chance to talk me out of it, or guilt trip me into sticking around. So I decided I would grit through the last few sessions, be all smiles and positivity until we took a break for Christmas and I would just ghost.

It was then he dropped a bombshell; he was going to compete.

He was putting his money where his mouth was. Not a local tournament though, no no, those were far too below him. He was aiming higher.

ADCC Trials.

Yup, his over-inflated ego eventually convinced him that he was good enough to win one of the toughest competitions on Earth, and then go on to win ADCC World Championships. I couldn't believe my ears. It was literally a done deal in his mind which, in a weird way, I kind of respect. The level of disillusion on display was so breathtaking I couldn't help but have a smidge of admiration for the confidence, albeit misguided.

This would eventually lead to his downfall.
By the time trials rolled around, I had sent a goodbye message into the group chat and informed the boys I wouldn't be continuing training. I told them I was sick of the gatekeeping and moving of the goalposts, and wanted to be taught by qualified instructors. This was passed onto him by one of the lads, who then passed on a voice note from MJ. He explained how confused he was, how he was looking forward to creating this Martial Art alongside me, a thinly veiled threat (is how I took it) of coming to my new gym for a roll blah blah. It made me laugh and further cemented my choice.

For those non-Jiu-Jitsu guys reading this - ADCC Worlds is considered the Everest of grappling; winning that competition would cement you in the top tier of the sport. It's where legends are made.

Trials are the qualifiers for the big show. Thousands of hungry athletes have trained their whole lives in the hope of running through the single elimination tournament to gain a single invite to the main event, held every two years. It is often considered harder than the main tournament itself.
I wasn't going to miss this.

When the event rolled around, our training group had dissipated pretty rapidly and many followed in leaving MJ in their past. We were however invested in seeing the conclusion to this story.

I bought a subscription to Flo Grappling and organised a watch party around my mate's house to see how this all played out. I cannot tell you what a wild ride of emotions those eight hours were - as we waited with baited breath constantly refreshing [Smooth Comp](#) to see when he was due to compete. Luckily, some incredible performances from talented players like [Levi Jones-Leary](#) would help pass the time.

To be honest I didn't even think he'd show up, that it was all a lie or he'd get cold feet. Credit where it's due, there he was, bald head bobbing around in the background of the live stream.

It was actually happening.

I wasn't sure how I felt. I remembered the way he treated me over the years, the damage he caused to my friends and strangers. The tyranny, the deceit and hypocrisy. It all came flooding back.

I wanted him to get hurt. I wanted a snapped arm. I craved blood.

Then I remembered the good that came from the experience. How, without him, I wouldn't have met any of the amazing, supportive men I am proud to call my friends. It was via his organisation that I was able to talk about my feelings for the first time. I was able to heal some, if not most, of my trauma through supportive groups of blokes who relived some of the most awful times of my life with me. With MJ's cult, I finally realised that life is worth living.

I remembered he was still a human, with faults and insecurities - despite his claims of enlightenment. Maybe I didn't want him to get hurt, I began to worry he might get injured and how devastating that could be.

I flipped back and forth between anger, worry, fear, joy and intrigue.

The time finally came. First round. He stood mat side as the ref called him up. After squatting down dramatically, one fist on the floor and sending a few prayers to the Moon, he strolled into the centre. His opponent was nowhere to be seen. Minutes passed, and still no show. MJ's hand was raised in a hollow bye victory, and he progressed to the next round by default.

I was pissed. We'd been waiting all day for this, watching incredible athletes fight for their lives and this tosser gets a free ride into round 2. Fuck, was everything going to fall in place for this guy? I began to doubt and wonder if he might actually manage to do this.

Crazier things have happened.

Another hour or so passed, and it was time for the second round. This time, his opponent was very much there. A guy called Moon - oh, the irony.

Out they went. MJ pulled guard instantly. His opponent stepped past his guard with ease and began to launch his smash offensive. MJ wriggled free and regained his guard. After some stalling from his opponent, a missed wrestle-up from MJ and a comical slip that made the cameraman giggle, they clashed on the floor again. He was getting dominated until Moon was in combat base, and MJ threaded his leg through to single leg X (or '3'). Their legs became entwined, and MJ hunted for the heel, which he soon found. His opponent f reed his knee line, rendering the heel hook ineffective, and MJ seemed a bit lost. His confidence seemed to be fading.

Another leg entanglement began, this time MJ left his foot dangling and unprotected as he looked for his submission. Moon jumped on his heel and began to crank a leg attack of his own, and that was all she wrote. MJ tapped.

He took a slow limp back to the centre, where his opponent was awarded the victory via heel hook.

And that was that.

Three minutes was all it took.

I don't really know how I felt at that moment. A mixture of relief that he didn't get his shit snapped. Relief also that I had made the correct decision to leave. I was also elated - this guy had been swanning about unopposed for years, enjoying the smell of his own farts for too long, and was finally humbled on the big stage. Thoroughly and definitively. And also a sense of emptiness as parts of me were able to let go of any resentment or anger I harboured.

I got closure. I had a brand <u>new gym</u> to continue my own Jiu-Jitsu journey. A gym full of supportive people who actively rebel against cult-like behaviour. It was time to leave MJ behind, once and for all.

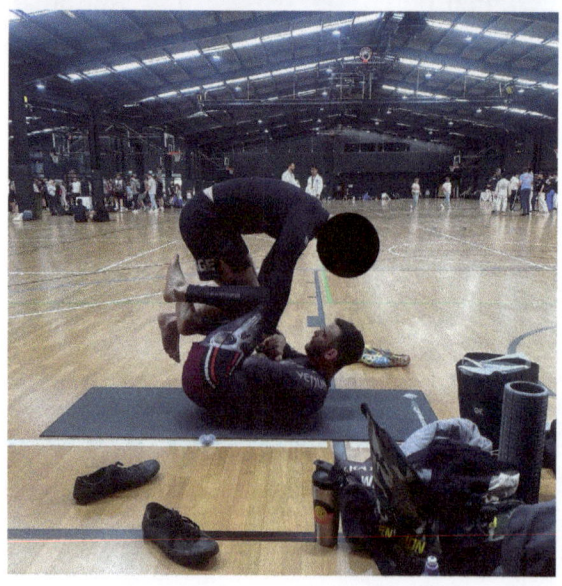

SUBSCRIBE TO
MARTIAL ARTS MAGAZINE AUSTRALIA

Australia's Only Ad-Free Martial Arts Magazine

Join our community and receive six issues over 18 months of authentic martial arts content—no advertisements, just pure dedication to the arts we love.

DIGITAL SUBSCRIPTION
$49.99
18 months • 6 issues
- PDF format delivered to your inbox
- Read on any device
- Instant access upon release
- Environmentally friendly

PRINT SUBSCRIPTION
$175.00
18 months • 6 issues
- High-quality print edition
- Delivered to your door
- Collector's quality
- Perfect for your library

Why Subscribe to MAMA?
✓ Ad-Free Content – No distractions, just martial arts
✓ Authentic Voices – Real practitioners sharing genuine insights
✓ Diverse Perspectives – Traditional and modern approaches across all styles
✓ Australian Focus – Celebrating our local martial arts community

Subscribe Today
Visit: www.martialartsmagazineaustralia.com
Email: info@martialartsmagazineaustralia.com

SUPPORT AUTHENTIC MARTIAL ARTS JOURNALISM IN AUSTRALIA

WRITE FOR US
Share Your Voice with Australia's Martial Arts Community

Martial Arts Magazine Australia is built on the voices of real practitioners—people who train, teach, compete, and live the martial arts every day. We're always looking for authentic stories, unique perspectives, and genuine insights from our community.

Whether you're a beginner sharing your first breakthrough, a seasoned instructor with decades of experience, or somewhere in between, we want to hear from you. Your story matters.

What We're Looking For
We welcome submissions across all martial arts styles and topics, including:
- Personal journeys and transformations
- Technical instruction and training methods
- Philosophy and the deeper meaning of martial arts
- Profiles of inspiring martial artists
- Historical and cultural perspectives
- Competition experiences and lessons learned
- Teaching insights and dojo management
- Women in martial arts
- Senior practitioners and lifelong learning
- Injury prevention and recovery
- Cross-training and integration of styles

What We Value
Authenticity over perfection. We want your real voice, not polished marketing speak. Share your genuine experiences, including the struggles and setbacks that make the victories meaningful.

Depth over superficiality. We're not interested in clickbait or surface-level content. Dive deep into your subject matter. Our readers appreciate substance.
Respect across traditions. Whether you practice traditional karate, modern MMA, or anything in between, all approaches deserve respect. We celebrate diversity without disparaging differences.

Contributor Benefits
Published contributors receive:
✓ A free 18-month digital subscription to MAMA (valued at $49.99)
✓ Author byline and bio with your photo and website/social media links
✓ Opportunity to reach Australia's martial arts community
✓ Professional editing support to help your article shine
✓ Publication in an ad-free environment where content comes first

Submission Guidelines
Article length: 800-3,000 words (we're flexible for exceptional content)
Format: Word document, Google Doc, or plain text
Images: High-resolution photos welcome (please confirm you have rights to use them)
Originality: Articles must be original and not previously published elsewhere
Author bio: Include a 2-3 sentence bio with your submission

The Process
1. Submit your article or pitch to info@martialartsmagazineaustralia.com
2. We'll review your submission within 7-10 business days
3. If accepted, we'll work with you on any edits or refinements
4. Your article will be scheduled for an upcoming issue
5. Upon publication, you'll receive your complimentary digital subscription

Not Sure Where to Start?
If you have an idea but aren't sure how to develop it, reach out to us. We're happy to discuss your concept and help you shape it into a compelling article. Sometimes the best stories come from conversations. Email us a brief description of your idea, and let's talk about how to bring it to life.

Your Voice Matters
Every martial artist has a unique perspective shaped by their training, their teachers, and their personal journey. We believe these diverse voices strengthen our community and enrich our understanding of the martial arts.

We look forward to hearing from you.
Submit Your Article or Pitch
Email: submissions@martialartsmagazineaustralia.com
Website: www.martialartsmagazineaustralia.com

www.ingramcontent.com/pod-product-compliance
Lightning Source LLC
Chambersburg PA
CBHW042026100526
44587CB00029B/4319